WOODEN TEMPLES
OF JAPAN

WOODEN TEMPLES OF JAPAN

Peter Popham

Photographs by Francesco Venturi

Tauris Parke Books, London

The author and photographer would like to thank the following for their help in the production of this book: His Excellency, the Italian Ambassador and his wife, Mr and Mrs Bartolomeo Attolico, Mr and Mrs Gianluigi Benedetti, Rika Kitagawa, Chigusa Ogino and Kiyohiko Tsukuda.

Published by Tauris Parke Books
110 Gloucester Avenue, London NW1 8JA
In association with KEA Publishing Services Ltd., London

TRAVEL TO LANDMARKS

Series Editor: Judy Spours
Editorial Assistant: Elizabeth Harcourt
Designer: David Robinson
Maps by John Hewitt
All photographs by Francesco Venturi except pages
13, 41, 42, 68, 103, Pacific Press Service, Tokyo.

British Library Cataloguing in Publication Data
Popham, Peter
   Wooden Temples of Japan. – (Travel to landmarks).
   1. Japan. Buddhist temples
   I. Title II. Series
   952

   ISBN 1-85043-175-2
   ISBN 1-85043-181-7 pbk

Photosetting by Litho Link Ltd., Welshpool, Powys, U.K.
Colour separation by Fabbri, Milan, Italy
Printed by Fabbri, Milan, Italy

FRONTISPIECE A view of the five-storey pagoda and other buildings in Horyuji, which are among the oldest wooden buildings in the world, probably dating from the end of the seventh century (see pages 36-8).

Contents

Regional Map of Japan   6

Introduction   9

1. The Native Tradition   19

2. The Coming of Buddhism   33

    Horyuji   33
Map of the Nara Region   34
    Yakushiji and Toshodaiji   43
    Kofukuji and Todaiji   50

3. Kyoto   61

Map of the Kyoto Region   62
    Kiyomizudera   66
    Toji and Saiji   70
    The Phoenix Hall of Byodo-in   73
    The rise of the warriors and the coming of Zen   77
    Nanzenji   81
    Daitokuji   88
    The Golden and Silver Pavilions   101

4. Kamakura and Beyond   105

Map of the Kamakura Region   108
    Architecture after Kamakura   115

    Travellers' Information   121

    Further Reading   124

    Index   125

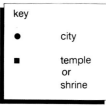

key

●   city

■   temple
        or
        shrine

REGIONAL MAP OF JAPAN

(Hokkaido and Okinawa are omitted)

SEA OF JAPAN

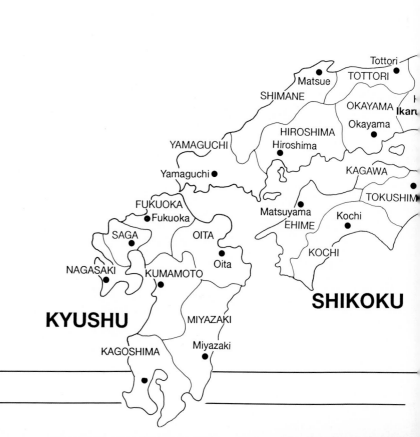

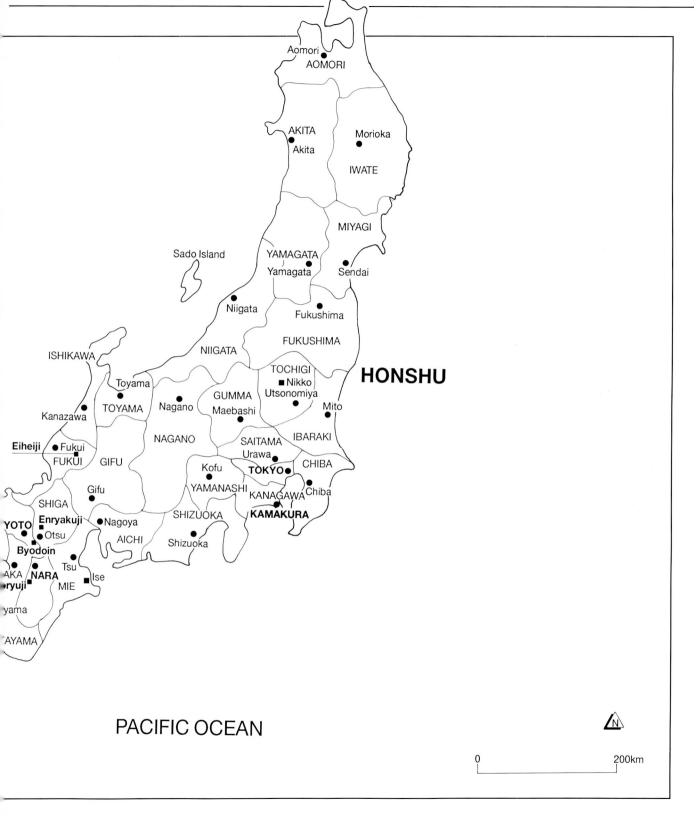

Aomori
AOMORI

AKITA
Akita

Morioka

IWATE

MIYAGI

Sado Island

YAMAGATA
Yamagata

Sendai

Niigata

Fukushima

FUKUSHIMA

NIIGATA

ISHIKAWA

Toyama

TOCHIGI
Nikko
Utsonomiya

HONSHU

TOYAMA

Nagano

GUMMA
Maebashi

Mito

Kanazawa

NAGANO

SAITAMA

IBARAKI

Eiheiji   Fukui
FUKUI   GIFU

Urawa

Kofu   TOKYO   CHIBA

Gifu

YAMANASHI   Chiba

SHIGA

Enryakuji   Nagoya

KANAGAWA
KAMAKURA

YOTO
Otsu

SHIZUOKA

Byodoin

AICHI   Shizuoka

Tsu

AKA   NARA
ryuji   MIE   Ise

yama

AYAMA

PACIFIC OCEAN

0   200km

Introduction

The story of the sacred architecture of Japan stretches back long before the start of the nation's recorded history and still continues today. It starts with the simple shrines of the native animistic cults that later came to be called Shinto; it continues today with new and reconstructed shrines and temples, with churches and cathedrals, and with the often bizarre buildings of the dozens of new religions that have sprouted during the past century.

This book does not pretend to be a survey of the whole field, which would require a volume the size of a telephone directory. Rather it is a selection of the most significant, the most interesting and the most beautiful religious buildings that were constructed during the long period when the religious impulse found its richest forms of expression.

Using these criteria, most of the buildings treated are Buddhist temples, and all of these were erected between the establishment of Buddhism in Japan in the sixth century, and the beginning of the Edo period a millennium later. The buildings which bracket the period of greatest interest are Horyuji, the monastery to the south of the city of Nara, and the mausoleum of the shogun Ieyasu at Nikko, north of Tokyo.

Ever since its founding in India, Buddhism made no bones about its concern with the way countries were governed and, from its first arrival in Japan, it was overtly political. Horyuji, which contains the world's oldest wooden buildings, was the handiwork of the regent Prince Shotoku, one of the most revered figures in Japanese history, and the author of the country's first constitution. He gave the alien religion the political as well as spiritual centrality which it was to retain for a thousand years. Shotoku's time was the heyday of Buddhism as a political force, in that there was complete identity between spiritual and secular authority. Never again would the relationship be so simple or so clean. The tension between the clerics and the governors first emerged at Nara a century later, when the construction of the nation's grandest temple, Todaiji, was followed with unseemly haste by the departure of the emperor and his court to a new location, to escape the priests' influence.

From then on it was a game of cat and mouse. The emperor who established Kyoto as capital attempted to put the priests in their place, relegating them to the role of guarding the city and confining their temples to the opposite end of it from the palace. But it wasn't long

ABOVE One wing of the most ornately decorated building in Japan, the mausoleum of Shogun Ieyasu at Nikko. It was constructed in a mere two years, between 1634 and 1636, by order of Iemitsu, grandson of Ieyasu, and was finished in time to mark the twentieth anniversary of the latter's death. Much of the decorative carving was the work of artisans from Korea.

RIGHT Garden of Zuishin-in temple in Kyoto. Autumn is the best season to visit Kyoto, when the flaming foliage makes a brilliant backdrop to the temples and stone gardens. The Japanese maple, *momiji*, its delicate leaves coloured deep crimson, is the tree most evocative of the season.

before new schools of Buddhism, the esoteric Tendai and Shingon sects, were jockeying for the position of intimate adviser to later emperors. As the glorious Heian period dissolved in decadence, it became a common spectacle to see armed bands of priests roaring down from their mountain-top headquarters to terrorize the capital and impose their will.

The last school of Buddhism to arrive from the continent and establish itself in the country was Zen, and this, too, made a direct and explicit bid to secure the favour of the country's rulers. It was successful: both the Hojo regents in Kamakura and the puppet emperors in Kyoto fell under its spell.

Ieyasu's mausoleum marks the end of this long, fevered period of intercourse between secular and religious power. Temples continued to be built, and the shoguns continued to patronize and pay for them. But no more schools arrived from the continent to enliven the scene intellectually, and Buddhism was replaced by Neo-Confucianism as the spiritual compass of the rulers. The Ieyasu mausoleum, in all its gaudy extravagance, co-opting for its own secular purposes the potent vocabulary of both Shinto and Buddhism, put an emphatic full stop to the long debate. The tension went out of the relationship, and with it the creative vigour with which it had developed new architectural styles.

The history of Buddhist architecture in Japan revives the endless and still momentous question about the Japanese: are they creators or copy-cats? Without attempting to impose a conclusion, it is worth pointing out that not only the initial input of Buddhist doctrine and paraphernalia but all its subsequent developments as well arrived fully formed from the continent. It was China where the new ideas were hammered out, the new sects created, the new fashions in building style and plan first formulated and perfected. So powerful were they that they not only determined the way that Buddhism developed in Japan, but also exerted a decisive influence on the architecture of Shinto. Chinese culture possessed a confidence, a definiteness and a courage in its convictions which the Japanese were never able to rival.

In Shotoku's time the Japanese mastered all the technical aspects of temple architecture, a tradition far superior in sophistication to anything indigenous. But they were capable of original work, too, and in the ages that followed they created masterpieces which rank with those of any

PREVIOUS PAGE Nandaimon, South Great Gate, of Todaiji in Nara, originally constructed in the mid-eighteenth century, was the crowning achievement of the first phase of the development of Buddhism in Japan. Burned down during civil strife in 1180, both the Buddha Hall and the gate which is its principal entrance were soon rebuilt in the 'Indian style' © Hiroshi Fujita.

ABOVE Lively and vivid depictions of animals crowd the exterior surfaces of buildings of the mid-sixteenth century, such as this, the Kara Mon ('Chinese Gate') of Nishi-Honganji temple in Kyoto. The style is in strong contrast to the usual Japanese preference for subdued tones and understatement.

BELOW FAR LEFT A sub-temple of Nanzenji, a great Zen temple of the Rinzai school in the north-east of Kyoto, established in the fourteenth century. The fine scale and delicate detailing of such gardens helps to balance the thundering grandeur of the temple's main buildings.

BELOW LEFT The pool and one of the wings of the Phoenix Hall of Byodo-in in Uji, south-east of Kyoto. The Phoenix Hall is the most beautiful surviving building of the Heian period. It was built in 1053 by Fujiwara Yorimichi, head of the powerful Fujiwara family, and was abandoned after their demise. It stood in ruins for many centuries, and was only restored in the 1950s.

religious tradition, east or west. Kyoto's Golden Pavilion and Silver Pavilion are famous examples, with their combination of delicacy and informality. The development of Zen in Japan illustrates how deference to continental models and radically original inspirations could coexist in a single institution. The main temple buildings of Zen were almost compulsively faithful to the Chinese pattern, but were surrounded with gardens, sub-temples, hermitages and living-quarters quite different from anything found on the continent. The tea cottage is perhaps the single most characteristic development: a direct offshoot of the Zen tradition, disarmingly humble in scale and style, yet informed by an aesthetic taste which went far beyond the rigid symmetrical forms typical of China.

Japanese taste achieved its apotheosis in the temples of Kyoto such as Daitokuji, Ryoanji and Nanzenji. But because Japan is the great storehouse of the architecture of the Far East it is also the best place to admire the more purely Chinese works. Most of the great temples of ancient China have long since disappeared, destroyed in successive waves of dynastic upheaval. Invasions and civil wars have been no kinder to the ancient architecture of Korea, where only those temples hidden away in obscure mountain passes have survived. But throughout all its history Japan was never invaded until the arrival of General MacArthur in 1945. It had plenty of petty civil wars, but little of the wholesale destruction which characterized such conflicts on the continent. One of the reasons for this difference has been the endurance of a single imperial house throughout the nation's history, a house which commanded loyalty – though at times only begrudging or token – of all the generalissimos who have wielded real power down the centuries.

Most of Japan's cities were razed to the ground in bombing raids during the last months of the Second World War. But even this apocalyptic destruction missed Kyoto, the city which has the richest and densest concentration of architectural masterpieces, and nearby Nara, where the only surviving examples from the age and in the style of China's T'ang dynasty are to be found.

Modern Japan has the most ephemeral and fast-changing cityscape of any country in the history of the world: return after an absence of six months and you lose your bearings because so many of the landmarks are gone. But by a strange paradox it is also a great museum of the changing architectural fashion from all periods of its history, stretching over some two thousand years. Nor are these monuments, like Java's Borabudur or Cambodia's Angkor Wat, the remains of a culture so remote from the lives of the people living today that a major effort of imagination is required to place them in a social context. Continuity in the midst of enormous change is the keynote of modern Japan. While the nation's best scientific brains throw themselves into the development of supercomputers or new applications of biotechnology, other young Japanese devote themselves assiduously to mastering the practical intricacies of temple carpentry as practised by their remotest ancestors. In the past ten years a new pagoda has been built at Yakushiji temple in Nara, using precisely the same techniques as those employed in the one it replaced, which burned down more than a thousand years ago.

Similarly, the most famous example of imperial domestic architecture, Katsura Rikkyu imperial villa, was recently renovated from top to bottom with the same painstaking attention to authenticity. Every twenty years, the holiest shrine of the indigenous Shinto religion, representing the highest attainment of Japanese architecture before the arrival of Buddhism, is reconstructed in the time-honoured way on a site adjacent to the one presently standing – which is then ceremonially destroyed. The next reconstruction is due to be completed in 1994.

For all these reasons, Japan is unrivalled as a place in which to experience directly the architectural achievements of one of the world's great nodes of civilization. This book is intended to be a companion to that experience. For those embarked or planning to embark on a trip to Japan, it provides a practical guide to what there is to see and how to see it. For them too, but also for those who do not seriously expect to have the chance to cross the world, it gives enough of the historical, cultural and architectural background behind the buildings to bring them to life.

A quintessential image of traditional Japan: the five-story eastern pagoda of Kofukuji temple, at 50 metres high the second tallest in the country, framed here by autumnal foliage. Kofukuji is one of the main temples in Nara Park, the best preserved concentration of historic architecture in the country.

1 The Native Tradition

At the shrines of Ise, the holiest in the country, the austere simplicity of the indigenous Shinto religion is maintained with few concessions to the architectural flamboyance which was introduced with Buddhism. In most shrines the *torii* entrance is painted vermilion: the ones at Ise are unpainted, and constructed in the simplest manner.

The Chinese taught the Japanese how to write, so the story of Japanese architecture before the arrival of Buddhism is inevitably rather hazy. What is clear and striking, however, is that both the materials and the modes of construction preferred by the Japanese for their houses were well established before the importation of Chinese culture began.

The traditional Japanese house, which as recently as 1979 was still favoured by 60 per cent of the house market, has all the insulating properties of a tent, and is just about as practical to keep warm. It is a cage of light wooden posts and beams. The walls between the posts, having no structural function, can be made of a variety of materials. Those on the outside are formed traditionally of a thin skin of lathe and plaster; most of those inside are composed either of stiffened paper (*fusuma*) or sheets of thin translucent paper stretched over a light wooden grid (*shoji*), and it is this that gave rise to the picturesque Western misconception that Japanese houses were actually constructed of paper. *Fusuma* and *shoji* are always removable, giving the Japanese house its famous flexibility – three or four small rooms can, with minimal effort, be transformed into a single large one. They are also the cause of its frigidity.

A variety of theories have been advanced to explain why the Japanese adopted and clung to this style of construction. Some are more fanciful than others. The idea that it was the legacy of early waves of immigration from south-east Asia, where similar building styles are favoured, no longer enjoys much academic support, owing to the paucity of hard evidence that immigrations of this sort actually occurred. The earthquake factor is clearly significant: many areas of Japan, including Tokyo, are frequently rocked by earthquakes, and a well-built post-and-beam house will sway and creak in a large quake but is less prone than brick actually to tumble down, and causes less damage if it does. Brick construction was widely adopted for offices, banks and other administrative buildings during the long wave of enthusiasm for all things Western during the Meiji period; many of them were shaken to pieces during the Great Kanto Earthquake of 1923, whereupon this style went out of fashion.

But the simplest explanation is probably the best: to build their houses the ancient Japanese used what was abundantly to hand, namely timber; and having arrived at a solution they liked, they stuck with it.

ABOVE LEFT Buildings in the pure
native style at Ise. The defining
features of the style are upward
extensions of the gables, called
katsuogi, and billets on the roof
ridge, called *chigi*.

ABOVE RIGHT Sprigs of the sacred
sakaki tree and sacred paper
fastened to an exterior column in
the Outer Shrine (*Geku*) of Ise. The
offering of greenery symbolizes the
first fruits of the harvest. Wands
made from this type of paper,
called *haraigushi*, are employed in
Shinto rituals of purification.

BELOW Shrine maiden in kimono
and crimson *hakama* (divided
skirts) at Ise's Outer Shrine. In
front of her is the box into which
visitors throw coins before praying.
The purple drapes are decorated
with stylized representations of
chrysanthemums, the symbol of the
imperial house.

The Japanese house is built for the summer, and in warm weather there is nothing to match it: breezes fan right through, the low eaves keep off the direct sun, and the sense of intimacy with the natural world outside, or the carefully orchestrated version represented by the garden, is unlike anything that can be experienced in houses built of heavier materials. Winter in such a house, by contrast, is a miserable, thoroughly chilling experience – though until the very recent past, when the Japanese began to travel in large numbers, that was only a problem for foreign visitors, as the Japanese themselves knew nothing different, and in any case had their own ways of keeping warm: hot sake, boiling baths and quantities of bedclothes. The story of house architecture in Japan invokes a theme which no book on Japanese culture can avoid for long: the conservatism of profound insularity.

However, the very earliest Japanese houses of which any evidence remains reveal an arguably more practical attitude to coping with the severity of the climate than has been fashionable since the Japanese learned to write. These are the pit-houses of the Jomon period, the culture which underwent its long, slow development during the third, second and first millennia BC. Archaeological findings suggest that the houses were between one metre and several centimetres deep, and roughly circular in plan. There was probably a central hearth, a superstructure of beams and a roof of thatch. Relatively cosy in winter, they would have been uncomfortably hot and sticky in the summer, and this might have induced their inhabitants to flee for the season to more satisfactory homes. Some of the evidence points in this direction – a note written around AD 300 by an inhabitant of Yamato, the plain where the city of Nara is located and the area from which the mainstream of Japanese culture sprang, says in unmistakably scornful tones of one of its aboriginal enemies that 'in winter they dwell in holes, in summer in nests'.

Jomon culture was overtaken in the final centuries BC by the relatively sophisticated Yayoi, who are more closely identifiable than the Jomon as forerunners of the present-day Japanese. Probably influenced by the architecture of the south coast of China, they lived in houses which are recognizably the ancestors of those of today, raised a short distance above the ground and built of a framework of posts and beams, probably topped off with roofs of thatch. Their appearance is preserved in pottery models from the fifth century AD and certain bronze engravings. On this evidence it appears that some of their houses had saddle-shaped roofs, others the combined hip and gable type, *irimoya* in Japanese, which has been popular ever since.

In other words, by the early centuries of this era the Japanese had arrived at an architectural idiom which satisfied them, and which was to constitute the firm foundation under the more sophisticated and fashion-driven styles which soon began entering from the continent. This form which was developed in the early Yayoi period is perpetuated today in the temporary shelters which are put up in farming areas at harvest-time. But it is also found in the holiest complex of buildings of the Shinto religion: the shrines of Ise. This is where the story of the sacred architecture of Japan truly begins.

Two religions have dominated Japan down the centuries: Shinto and Buddhism. Shinto is usually called Japan's indigenous religion, though it has many points in common with the shamanism practised on the Korean peninsula. It is a vast agglomeration of superstitions, animistic beliefs and customs. Until the appearance in the country of its rival, Buddhism, it did not even have the token integration bestowed by a unifying name. Shinto simply means 'the Way of the Gods', to distinguish it from Butsu-do, 'the Way of the Buddha'.

Shinto is a primitive religion, possessing a wonderful profusion of gods and spirits but without any doctrine or philosophical apparatus. The *kami*, 'gods' (which is not really an adequate translation) can be anything which inspires people with awe – anything from an erupting volcano to a crafty fox, from a barbarian-subduing generalissimo to a curiously shaped tree. Wherever a *kami* is identified, at the bottom of a waterfall, for example, or the foot of a wooded hill, there a shrine is built. In essence it is a home for the *kami*. From the most elaborate to the simplest, there are many thousands to be found across the country.

Though it lacks ideas, Shinto does not lack a creation myth. As recorded in *kojiki*, Japan's oldest book, the *Record of Ancient Things*, it is very complicated but great fun, and centres around the tale of how the Sun Goddess, who had plunged the world into darkness by retreating into a cave to sulk, was lured out again by a striptease performance. It was the vigorous offspring of this goddess who, according to the story, peopled Japan and civilized it. Their remote descendant was the Emperor Jimmu, who established the dominion of his people over the archipelago, supposedly in about 600 BC.

Japan's imperial family has never been supplanted, so according to the story the present emperor, Akihito, is himself a descendant of the Sun Goddess. The Inner Shrine at Ise, regarded as more sacrosanct than the nearby Outer Shrine, is dedicated to that mythical ancestress, Ameterasu-Omikami, and the emperor and other members of the imperial family visit on set occasions to commune with her and inform her of important changes. This shrine also houses the three holy symbols of the imperial house, the mirror, sword and jewel. The Outer Shrine, only slightly less awe-inspiring to believers than the Inner, is dedicated to Toyouke-Omikami, the goddess of farms, harvest, food and sericulture. For the foreign visitor, the shrines at Ise are among the most moving and interesting places in the whole of Japan. They are moving because, although all but the outermost of the four fences which protect the holy objects are closed to the public, the atmosphere of sanctity, reinforced by the immaculate condition in which the richly forested site is maintained, is as palpable as that of any Christian cathedral. They are interesting because they give a very good idea of the point to which the native architecture had developed when it was inundated by influence from the continent.

One of the main preoccupations of Shinto is with ritual purity. It was to avoid pollution and keep themselves pure that, before the arrival of Chinese influence, the imperial family moved the capital to a new site every time an emperor died, because the worst pollution of all is death. So ingrained was the habit that even after they had accepted in theory the Chinese idea of a permanent capital, they changed its location as many as nine times before settling down for good in Kyoto. This same impulse – the rejection of dirt, decay and infection – was responsible for the extraordinary custom of destroying the Ise shrines every twenty years, and rebuilding an exact copy on an adjacent site. The stupendous investment of energy and resources which this custom represents leads some authorities to doubt that it could really have been carried out punctiliously all down the centuries. But it certainly is today.

There are other shrines in Japan which go back as far as those at Ise or even farther. The most famous is Izumo Taisha, in present-day Shimane Prefecture on Honshu's north-west coast, facing Korea. Its foundation is described in one of the other ancient books of tales of Japanese prehistory, the *Nihon Shoki*, in which it is told how the Sun Goddess herself built the shrine for her nephew, Onamochi. Certainly

PREVIOUS PAGE Pond garden of the Outer Shrine at Ise in early autumn.

Roofs of shrine buildings in Ise's Outer Shrine, showing the *chigi* billets on the ridges. Scholars hypothesize that they were originally used in primitive buildings to help anchor the roof, but at Ise they have long ceased to have any practical function, and are now considered one of the symbols of Shinto architecture at its purest.

Elaborate, Chinese-influenced
design motifs seen in the public
buildings of Ise's Inner Shrine
(*RIGHT*), and Outer Shrine
(*ABOVE*). Both exhibit the curved
gable beloved of Edo period
architects; that of the Inner Shrine
is doubled, and extends over a
broader flight of steps.

Detail of the roof of one of the Edo-style buildings at Ise, the voluptuous curves contrasting starkly with the stiff simplicity of the orthodox shrine style exemplified by the shrine's more sacred buildings.

its foundation goes back deep into the mists of time, and its simple plan reflects its venerable age: the sanctuary building is in form a simple gabled box just two bays wide with the entrance to the right of the axial pillar reached by stairs. But like most Shinto shrines in the country, its design has been powerfully influenced by later architectural developments. The present incarnation dates from 1744, and presents a much less pure and plausible image of Japan's earliest sacred architecture than Ise.

Ise preserves its primeval simplicity almost intact. The Inner Shrine is said to have been first built in the late third century AD on the instruction of Emperor Suinin. According to the *Nihon Shoki*, there had been a terrible and unexplained plague during the reign of his predecessor, Emperor Sujun, and in his panic the emperor conceived a dread of all unseen powers, even including his divine ancestors the Sun Goddess and the divine spirit of the land who rejoiced in the name Yamato-no-okunidama-no-kami. Until that time they had been worshipped together in the great hall of his palace, but he had their sanctuaries removed to a safe distance. Under his successor, Suinin, this arrangement was made perfect, the first two shrine buildings were erected, and the emperor appointed his daughter to be the high priestess of the shrine to the Sun Goddess. The Outer Shrine was established a couple of centuries later, towards the end of the fifth century, by the emperor Yuryaku. These shrines were so central to the most important pieties of the religion that they proved all but immune to the changes in architectural fashion which swept over the rest of the country down the ages. Accordingly, the buildings which visitors will glimpse after the ceremonial unveiling in 1994 will be both the newest and the most ancient in the country.

The first thing to say about them, however, is that they are not very special. They represent a sort of apotheosis of the primitive Japanese farmhouse. Yet they are executed with the infinite care and skill and devotion which might be lavished on a vastly expensive and delicate piece of jewellery. It is this combination of primitiveness of design and perfection of execution which makes a visit such a poignant experience. Like the storehouses of the Yayoi period which they closely resemble, the Ise buildings are raised on stilts. In the old storehouses this was to keep out the rats. The structure is straightforward, and clearly expressed. Fat round posts intersect with square beams; the walls, in contrast to the wattle-and-daub of Buddhist architecture, are made of horizontal planks. The roof is of thick, dark brown thatch, so smooth and consistent in texture it looks as if it was made in a Japanese factory. The roofline is the single element that speaks most strongly of Ise's pre-Chinese date, because there is no upswinging curve to it. At either end of the roof are strange beams, projecting upwards like extensions of the gables which the carpenters had omitted to cut off, while heavy cylindrical wooden billets are interspersed along the ridge. The former are called *chigi* – and no one knows what they were originally meant for. The latter are called *katsuogi*, and it is speculated that they were originally put there to help stop the roof blowing away in strong winds. Both have long outlived their respective functions, however, and have become symbolic of Shinto in general and of Ise in particular.

Ise's priests and officials have protected its Japanese virginity down the ages, but even here, despite their watchfulness, certain continental influences have crept in. The *shoden*, or sanctuary, for example, has a railed balcony running around it, and ornamental bronze covers over the protecting ends of the beams, Buddhist-influenced details added to the design during the Edo period. The gentle downward curve of the thatch is likewise thought to be a sophistication of the roof's original look.

But these corruptions are trivial compared to what has happened to the Izumo Taisha shrine. The box-like form of the sanctuary is authentically primitive, but the long graceful curve of the roof is unmistakably Chinese. The *chigi* have been moved in from the gable and now perch comically near the middle of the ridge-pole looking like oversize scissors. The *katsuogi* look equally unstable and pointless, balanced precariously on a ridge-pole which itself has a distinctly Chinese look.

It is interesting that even at the heart of Shinto, there is so little to be found that is truly pure. It is a measure of the seductive potency of the new influences arriving from the continent. So ravishing was that storm of intellectual and aesthetic novelty, it is surprising that the old forms and practices were not swept away altogether.

Roofline of sanctuary building at Ise with one of the massive zelkova trees which are found in abundance here in the background.

2

The Coming of Buddhism

One of the giant guardian (*Nio*) figures at the entrance to Horyuji, the Buddhist monastery established south of present-day Nara City by Prince Shotoku, the father of Japanese Buddhism, in 607. As in most temples of whatever date, the figures stand in niches to the right and left of the temple's main entrance, one with its mouth open, the other closed, to keep away evil spirits.

Nara and Kyoto, the two great pre-modern centres of Japanese civilization, contain hundreds of temples from every period of their history. They can be identified by the suffix *-ji*, which means temple, or occasionally by *-tera* or *-dera*, which is the alternative, indigenous way of reading the same Chinese character. Although each temple is in some sense a centre of Buddhist worship, their differences are far more striking than their similarities. There are the fragile, doll's-house-like structures of the Silver Pavilion and the Golden Pavilion, the expansive grounds of Daitoku-ji and Nanzen-ji, dotted with smaller sub-temples and hermitages and their private gardens, the bombast of Nishi-Honganji and Higashi-Honganji, the mighty cathedrals in Japan's age of Buddhism for the masses, whose founder's halls can swallow up thousands of believers at a time.

Each type of temple represents a different way in which the initial Buddhist message, architectural as well as doctrinal, was interpreted down the centuries. They are like a thousand streams, the character of each stream formed by the geology through which it travels. The great ancestor of them all, the spring from which, in a sense, they all sprang, is a monastery in the plain of Yamato, south of Nara, called Horyuji.

Horyuji

Out on its own among the paddies in a place called Ikaruga, a half-hour bus journey from the dense cluster of temples and shrines in Nara itself, Horyuji contains the oldest wooden buildings in the world. As a monastic centre it lost its vitality many centuries ago, but it preserves the monastic form and atmosphere. Most of the temples of Nara and Kyoto are so ancient that, on first inspection, all feel equally remote from us in time. Yet, even on first acquaintance, the broad, dusty spaces of Horyuji, the symmetrical plan, the extraordinarily well-preserved library and refectory and pagoda, somehow feel decidedly more archaic.

Japan had had intermittent contacts with the continent, and particularly with the independent states which squabbled for mastery of the Korean peninsula, throughout the early centuries of the Christian era. But as China approached that zenith of power and achievement which was the T'ang dynasty, when its court, receiving envoys from all over the known world, became a cauldron of cultural exchange, contacts between Japan and China increased in step. In the sixth

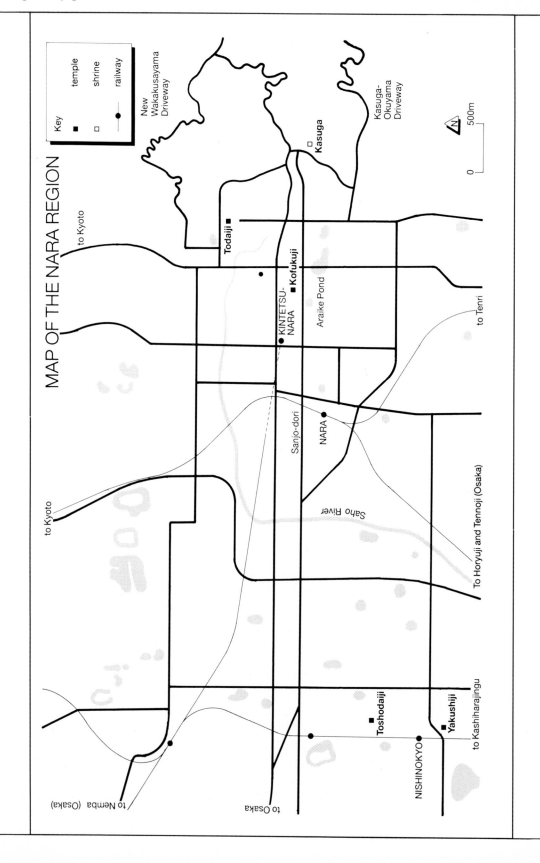

MAP OF THE NARA REGION

Key
temple ■
shrine □
railway ●—●

New Wakakusayama Driveway

Kasuga-Okuyama Driveway

□ **Kasuga**

N

0 500m

to Kyoto

Todaiji ■

Kofukuji ■

KINTETSU-NARA ●

Araike Pond

to Tenri

Sanjo-dori

NARA ●

Saho River

to Kyoto

To Horyuji and Tennoji (Osaka)

Toshodaiji ■

Yakushiji ■

NISHINOKYO ●

to Kashiharajingu

to Nemba (Osaka)

to Osaka

century the Yamato court formed an alliance with Paekche, the southwest Korean state, and it is said that it was in order to strengthen the bond that, in 552, the King of Paekche presented his island allies with what turned out to be a profoundly seminal gift: 'an image of the Buddha Sakyamuni in gilded bronze', according to the *Nihon Shoki*, 'with several banners and canopies, and a number of scrolls of canonical books'.

For a generation the alien religion did not take hold, and instead the whole question of foreign influence became – not for the last time – a raging controversy. Civil war flared, but the xenophobes lost it, and as a result Japan's first great craze for foreign culture got under way. It is fair to say that, once they are convinced of the rightness of a particular course of action, the Japanese do not do things by halves. The wave of continental influence initiated by Paekche's gift was not to stop until practically every aspect of Japanese life had been transformed by it.

Japan's first great patron of Buddhism was Prince Shotoku, who was regent during the reign of the Empress Suiko, from 593 till his own death in 622. It was under Shotoku's patronage that Horyuji was built, in the region that was home to his favourite consort. With its study and teaching facilities and its shifting communities of monks, it was one of the most important points of dissemination for the new religion. Completed in 607, it burned to the ground sixty-three years later. Exactly when it was rebuilt is unclear, but evidence from the detailing of the extant building suggests it was not long after the fire.

More than a millennium later Horyuji narrowly escaped being destroyed again, ironically during yet another explosion of enthusiasm for foreign culture. This was during the Meiji period which followed the downfall of the shogunate in the late 1860s, and the culture in question was not Chinese but Western. The passion for all things Western resulted in a feeling of disdain for Japan's traditional culture, and Horyuji, now regarded as a pointless old relic, was sold outright to a local public bath operator for use as fuel. The deal was only stopped at the last moment by the intercession of a scholarly foreigner.

The core of Horyuji consists of an inner gate, a pagoda and Golden Hall alongside each other enclosed by a corridor, and a lecture hall beyond the corridor to the north. The side-by-side alignment of Golden Hall and pagoda is a probably unique solution to the chief problem of temple design in Chinese and Japanese practice: what to do with the pagoda? Although Buddhism was in origin an Indian religion, the Chinese clothed it in unambiguously Chinese architecture once they had embraced it, and the design of Chinese temples was very similar to that of palaces and other important public buildings. The only important differences was the inclusion of a pagoda, the Chinese interpretation of the original Indian *s'tupa*, the tower at the base of which were preserved the historical Buddha's relics. The pagoda was therefore the holiest spot in the temple compound, but it was also an alien element which the otherwise purely Chinese plan had a great deal of trouble accommodating. Put in pride of place, on an axis with the entrance, it obscured and diminished the other buildings beyond, including the Buddha Hall, whose images rivalled the pagoda's relics in sacred importance. Put to one side and two pagodas became necessary, according to the strict Chinese rules of symmetry, which in turn diminished them, making them more like enormous ornaments. The history of Buddhist architecture in Japan is in a sense a series of answers to the question: What to do with the pagoda?

The simplest solution is seen at Shittenoji in Osaka which still retains its ancient, original plan, despite having been destroyed and rebuilt many times since its first construction in 588. Like all the temples of this early period, the approach was from the south, through the Nandaimon or South Great Gate. Beyond that was another gate, and beyond, still in a straight line, the towering bulk of the pagoda. This powerful single axis continued right through to the Lecture Hall at the back of the compound. But it was not an answer that can have satisfied the bonzes who had to pray and teach in the tower's shadow, and several other configurations were tried before what is certainly the craftiest solution was hit on: taking the pagoda right outside the temple compound altogether and sitting it down in a spectacular natural setting, halfway up a forested mountainside for example, where the pleasing harmony of the pagoda and the ingredients from which it was fashioned could be enjoyed by passing pilgrims.

The solution at Horyuji is one of the most curious of any. Placing the two sacred elements, pagoda and Buddha Hall, alongside each other, made their rivalry for pre-eminence explicit, but this ambiguity was resolved by making it the motif governing the layout of the whole central area. The central axis passing between pagoda and Buddha Hall is made a blind one. The Inner Gate giving on to the central courtyard

View of the five-storey pagoda and other buildings in Horyuji, which are among the oldest wooden buildings in the world, probably dating from around the end of the seventeenth century. The five roofs of this pagoda diminish in size gradually from bottom to top, contributing to its great sense of stability. Despite its imposing size, the building's only function is to contain relics of the historical Buddha. No use is made of the spaces above the ground.

ABOVE FAR LEFT Another view of Horyuji's pagoda.

ABOVE NEAR LEFT Plastered wall and ornamental rooftiles at Horyuji Temple, south of Nara.

BELOW LEFT Lecture Hall of Horyuji with the inevitable phalanx of schoolboys lined up in front of it in their Prussian-style black uniforms. Schools all over Japan make expeditions to the famous sites of Kyoto and Nara to familiarize students with the key masterpieces of their culture.

ABOVE Detail of Horyuji's pagoda, showing the characteristic, simple bracketing technique used all over this temple, which was superseded by more sophisticated and robust methods in the centuries to come. The bracket arms are distinguished by the cloud-like patterns carved in them. The ornamental vertical strut at the corner was added in the Edo period to strengthen the cantilever.

consists of three bays but has only two openings, at left and right, the central one being blocked. This curious arrangement has a plausible explanation. In its original incarnation, the temple was located some distance away from its present site. In the fire which consumed it in 670, only the Kondo, the Buddha Hall, which was some way removed from the rest of the temple, survived. The image housed in this hall had been cast in 623 as a prayer for the recovery of Prince Shotoku from his final illness, so after his death the building became his mortuary chapel. Its miraculous survival of the fire and its close link to the temple's founder meant that when the temple was reconstructed it was bound to become the core building. There was a difficulty, however: the other survivor of the fire had been the former temple's principal Buddha image – but this was now homeless, its hall having been destroyed. The solution was to build a new Buddha Hall in which the two images would be displayed side by side, neither one taking precedence. In this way the theme of the dual axis was brought about. It was then duplicated on a huge scale by the dual image of pagoda and Buddha Hall alongside each other.

Apart from its heroic and ancient architecture, Horyuji is also a fabulous museum of Asuka period art (552–645). The bronze image of Shakyamuni, the historical Buddha, in the Golden Hall is the image that was made at the time of Shotoku's last illness. It was the work of Japan's first great sculptor, Tori, whose family had immigrated from Korea in 522. Alongside it is the statue of Yakushi, the Buddha of Medicine, which survived the fire that consumed the hall it originally stood in, and which was by the same hand. There are many other great works of art in Horyuji. In the Yumedono Hall is a wooden statue of Kannon, divinity of mercy, which is extraordinarily lifelike despite the stiff, stylized sculpting of the drapes, and with a face full of kindness and sweetness. The paintings in the Tamamushi Zushi, the 'Beetle-wing Shrine', date from about the same period, the early seventh century. Not only are these the oldest paintings in Japan, but they are the only representatives of the painting of the period which have survived. Done in lacquer, they represent Bodhisattvas, pagodas and scenes of devotion such as the Sacrifice to a Hungry Tigress. There are also narrative scenes taken from the Jakata stories, depicting the virtuous deeds accomplished by the Bodhisattvas and how they managed to attain Buddhahood as a result. The Bodhisattvas are tall, lean and austerely

The 13-storied pagoda of Tanzan Shrine in Nara. The shrine was originally built in the seventh century, but this pagoda, the shrine's symbol and designated an Important Cultural Property, dates from 1451. All 13 roofs are thatched with cypress bark. Photo © Takeji Iwamiya.

Yakushiji at Nishinokyo, west of Nara proper. First built in 680 and originally one of the most important temples in the capital, the buildings of Yakushiji are presently under reconstruction in the most ambitious rebuilding project of the age, scheduled for completion in 2030. Photo © Hiroshi Fujita.

OVERLEAF LEFT The huge image of Vairocana, the Cosmic Buddha, 'the sun whose light reaches the darkest corners of the universe and yet leaves no shadow anywhere', located in the Buddha Hall of Todaiji, the largest wooden building in the world. The bronze statue, which dates from the late eighth century, took two years to cast and three more to polish and gild, and is nearly fifteen metres tall.

OVERLEAF TOP RIGHT Front view of Todaiji's Buddha Hall, showing the prominent golden commas on the roof and the curved hood over the entrance, between the two roofs – an inspiration of the architect who rebuilt the hall in the Edo period. Though much smaller than in its original form, which burned down in the twelfth century, the Buddha Hall is still massively imposing, and dominates much of Nara Park.

OVERLEAF BOTTOM RIGHT The curved hood of the Buddha Hall of Todaiji in Nara: in shape it is strikingly suggestive of a samurai helmet.

sensuous in a way that is strongly reminiscent of the statuary of the same period.

The Guardian Kings of the Four Quarters which stand on the central altar of Horyuji date from around the middle of the seventh century and are distinguished by the extremely unrealistic, schematic handling of the edges of the garments, but also by the lifelike proportions and mood of the figures themselves; Bishamonten, for example, who stands on a bizarre-looking demon with a disarmingly matter-of-fact expression on his face. Quite different and not to be missed is the Kudara (Korean) Kannon, an elongated figure of breath-taking elegance which may, as its name suggests, have actually been imported from Korea. Even more famous is the Miroku (Buddha of the Future) which is to be found at Chugu-ji, immediately to the east of Horyuji. This nunnery was originally the home of Shotoku's mother and was made into a temple after her death. The sleekly shining Miroku was carved from camphor wood. The right leg is crossed over the left thigh, right elbow rests on the right knee, the right index finger poised on the chin as the Buddha meditates on human suffering. In Buddhist teaching this is the Bodhisattva who disdains full enlightenment until all sentient beings attain salvation, whereupon he becomes the second and last Buddha, following Shakyamuni, to appear on earth. Suffering is his lot, but never was it borne with such patient detachment as is evinced by this figure.

Yakushiji and Toshodaiji

Another of the most important temples in the Nara area is Yakushiji, built in about 680, probably only a few years after the reconstruction of Horyuji, although it was moved to its present site in 720. But the differences between Horyuji and Yakushiji are striking. To go directly from one to the other is to gain a vivid impression of the speed at which temple design was developing during this period.

For one thing, Yakushiji is much larger. There is nothing here of the older temple's cloistered intimacy; instead, we find the first intimations of the fierce Japanese ambition to match and surpass the achievements of the Chinese, an ambition that was finally realized in Todaiji.

At Yakushiji the pagodas are pulled to either side, doubled and thereby rendered gigantically ornamental. They stand like huge sentinels at the extreme right and left through the main gate. Arcane

controversy has surrounded these particular specimens ever since they were built: the question of whether they are really of three storeys or six. Each has six roofs, to be sure, but only three are primary ones. Those in between are shallower and narrower, the upper ones an echo of the arrangement on the ground floor, where the inclusion of a secondary roof closer to the ground enabled the architect to give the building a larger ground plan than would have been possible otherwise. In fact this double roof technique is the dominant motif at Yakushiji, rather as the placing of elements of equal value alongside each other was the theme of Horyuji: the Buddha Hall embodies the same idea, with a shallower penthouse below the building's two great primary roofs. Examination of either Horyuji or Yakushiji fills one with admiration for the way in which in each place the designer allowed each building to play its subtle part in the integrated whole – although the design of Yakushiji's pagoda has been criticized for awkwardness, and was never repeated.

Coming to Yakushiji from Horyuji brings another vital development into focus, that of the bracketing which supports the roofs of these buildings. At Horyuji this key detail of temple design is still at a primitive stage, with an arm projecting perpendicularly from the square capital at the top of each column into the aisle to support the end of the roof beam. The underside of each of these arms is supported by a corbel in which cloud designs have been cut. The two-dimensional quality and the linear elaboration of this design accord perfectly with the forms of the buildings, and it is of a piece with the sculpture of the period. But it is lacking in robustness, particularly at the corners, where there is an alarming look of frailty about the single arm which supports a wide purlin span. In an eighteenth-century renovation, new pillars were prudently inserted at the corners to forestall any possible collapse.

At Yakushiji, by contrast, the brackets have taken on the muscular look which has since come to epitomize temple bracketing, and which with minor variations was to survive all the fluctuations in temple design of the succeeding centuries. The arm projecting from the capital at the top of each column has three heads into which the transverse beam above notches, and another arm projecting outwards whose head supports another arm. The head of that third arm supports the end of the beam which slices down from the roof, while that beam in turn supports a three-headed arm into which the purlin above notches. The

ABOVE Side view of Todaiji's Buddha Hall and garden.

BELOW One of a number of statues of priests who were active in the early history of Todaiji. This one is located just outside the temple's Buddha Hall and has been adorned with a bib and cap by pious visitors.

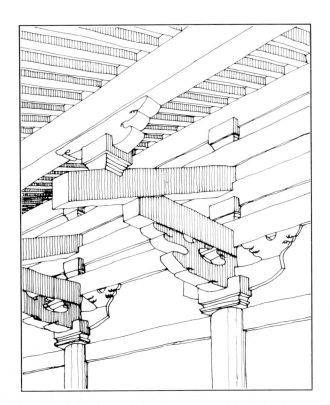
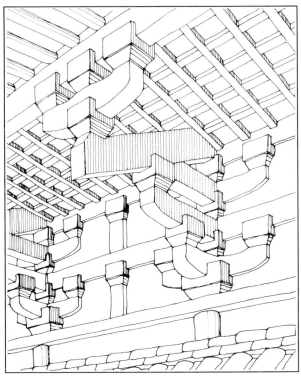

The design of temple bracketing developed rapidly. (*LEFT*) Relatively primitive seventh-century bracketing at Horyuji; (*RIGHT*) far more robust and complex work at Yakushiji constructed in the eighth century.

Jizo, god of children, is one of the most popular Buddhist deities in Japan, and perhaps the only one which originated in the country. His images are frequently found by the side of the road, where, like this one at Kofukuji in Nara, they are kept clean and well supplied with offerings by the local parishioners.

result is great security and strength.

Until recently the only building in the Yakushiji complex which retained its original appearance was the eastern pagoda. All the other buildings had been destroyed or replaced by anachronistic substitutes. In the single most impressive renovation of the present age, however, and after intensive study by archaeologists and other experts, the temple is now being restored to its original condition. Already the western pagoda, the Buddha Hall and the Picture Hall have been rebuilt. Work is now going ahead on other structures in the enormous grounds, and the whole project is scheduled for completion in 2030. Ongoing work is the explanation for the iron sheds off to the right of the buildings which are now standing: the reconstruction of the temple's component buildings goes on under cover. This great undertaking makes the quiet, rustic corner of Nara where Yakushiji is located, a short distance away from Nishinokyo ('western capital') station on the private Kintetsu Line, even worthier of a visit than it was before. It is one of those parts of Japan, sadly rare, where a serious attempt has been made to preserve the historical beauty of the setting, and the new towers of Yakushiji rise above small farmhouses with half-timbered walls and heavy roof tiles, the sort of scenery that has been customary here for hundreds of years. A ten-minute walk from Yakushiji to the north stands the temple of Toshodaiji. While much more modest in scale than Yakushiji, in its way it is one of the most beautiful monuments of the age of Nara's greatness, the Tempyo era.

Toshodaiji was built at the command of a great Chinese missionary called Chien-chên, Ganjin in Japanese, who is one of the most revered figures in the early history of Buddhism in Japan. He was invited to the country by the emperor, but his arrival was long delayed: he made five unsuccessful attempts at crossing during a period of twelve years before finally arriving at Nara in AD 754, by which time his eyesight had been destroyed by disease. He had an ordination temple erected in front of the greatest temple in the land, Todaiji, and personally instructed two emperors, Shoma and Koken, as well as many priests, in the higher mysteries of the religion. Toshodaiji was the temple to which he retired in 759, dying there five years later. The temple possesses a famous statue of Ganjin meditating, but it is only put on public display once a year, on 6 June.

Through Toshodaiji's recently reconstructed South Great Gate one comes directly to the temple's famous Buddha Hall, the largest surviving example from the eighth centre and a masterpiece of strength and simplicity which has been compared to the Parthenon. The bracketing reveals an increase in strength and confidence even beyond that achieved at Yakushiji, and a breath-taking advance on Horyuji. Noteworthy among the other dozen or so structures spread across the landscaped site are log-cabin-type repositories in the *azekura* style, identical in structure to the much more famous (and larger) Shosoin storehouse at Todaiji, and said to be even older.

Toshodaiji has many wooden images dating from the period of its construction, in the style introduced by the Chinese craftsmen who accompanied Ganjin to Japan. The most famous is the majestic 1000-armed Kannon – in actual fact there are said to be 953 arms – which is some five and a half metres tall.

Kofukuji and Todaiji

Two of the most important Buddhist establishments in the country, Kofukuji and Todaiji, are to be found in Nara proper. Founded in 710 as Heijo-kyo, 'capital of the peaceful citadel', this was the fourth attempt at creating a permanent, Chinese-style capital in sixty-five years – and as it lasted until 740, it can be considered a comparative success. Like the Chinese capital it imitated, it was laid out in a strict grid, and it is the blocks within the grid occupied by the city's most important temples and shrines which constitute the present-day Nara Park. Arguably it is the most attractive concentration of temples and shrines in the country, the ancient buildings connected by lawns kept closely cropped by the deer which wander free, protected since ancient times as messengers of the gods. To the east are steep wooded hills. Here as in the Nishinokyo area the most jarring reminders of modern Japan have been banished; power lines are underground, the few shops and houses are diminutive and in the best archaic taste, and the modern Japanese tourists walk through it all in their jeans and skirts like visitors from a different and unrelated civilization.

The first complex reached on arrival in the city is Kofukuji, which was built between 710 and 730. It was originally constructed fifty years earlier on the estate of the top Fujiwara family, in what is now Kyoto Prefecture. When Nara became the capital, this was the first temple to be relocated in it. Kofukuji's intimate ties with the Fujiwara, for many

ABOVE The *Nanendo* or Southern Octagonal Hall of Kofukuji in Nara, one of the stops on a popular pilgrimage route in western Japan. It illustrates well the deep interpenetration of Buddhist and Shinto practices in Japan, for although this is part of an ancient Buddhist temple, the rope hanging down in the middle of the picture is shaken to ring the gong at the top to awaken the attention of the god enshrined here – a purely Shinto custom.

BELOW Detail of Nanendo, showing the god-arousing gong and a pious text in the calligraphy of one of the temple's early worthies, preserved in gold.

centuries the nation's *de facto* second family, show the close interpenetration of political and religious power in this period. The temple was allocated four blocks in the capital, half the number reserved for the imperial palace. Kofukuji also represents another step in the rapid marginalization of the pagoda. As at Yakushiji, it is removed from the central axis and doubled: but here the two pagodas are outside the confines of the complex altogether, as defined by the Southern Great Gate. The eastern, five-storey pagoda is the second highest in the country at about fifty metres, and the latest reconstruction was in 1415. The delicate three-storey pagoda on the west dates from the early twelfth century.

Kofukuji is home to many splendid statues of the Nara period which somehow survived the numerous fires and are now housed in the *kokuho-kan* (museum), east of the Central Golden Hall. A number of the most precious, notably the Hachibu-shu or Group of Guardians, are executed in the dry-lacquer technique popular at the time, in which a clay inner core was wrapped with several layers of hemp cloth soaked in lacquer; that surface was coated in lacquer and then carved. The robust realism of the images is striking.

The temple's buildings present a venerable enough appearance, but nothing survives from the original construction. The present buildings date from the thirteenth century and after, but they retain their original organization, and the Northern Octagonal Hall in particular, an architectural feature strongly evocative of T'ang period sophistication, is close in form to the original, as it was constructed on the original stone base.

Kofukuji is a popular place with tourists and pilgrims alike. The temple's Nanendo or Southern Octagonal Hall is temple number nine on west Japan's Thirty-three Temple pilgrimage route. Japanese Buddhism is often described as moribund, its chief remaining role the cremation of the dead, but if this is so it is hard to explain the continuing popularity of pilgrimages. A steady stream of pilgrims passes through the temple's grounds, armed with their walking sticks and prayer beads, stopping before the Nanendo to awaken the god's attention by pulling on the multi-coloured rope that rattles the rusty-sounding gong. Next to it is the small hall of Hitokoto Kannon, relocated here during the Meiji period. Its name means 'Single-utterance Kannon' in reference to the belief that merely by speaking the

Buddha's name once, a response is assured. Most of the pilgrims pause here to pull the bell rope, light a candle or a stick of incense, then line up at the window next door where, for 200 yen, an attendant executes the magnificently ornate piece of calligraphy which serves as proof of the pilgrim's visit.

In front of the Hitokoto Kannon luxuriates a magnificent growth of wisteria, especially beautiful in the spring, when it is in flower. This is a reminder of the temple's origins, because the Japanese for wisteria is *fuji*, and it is the symbol of the Fujiwara family. There's more wisteria up the road at the Kasuga Taisha shrine, for this place too is tightly linked to the Fujiwaras. It was home to the family's *ujigami* or tutelary deity. Like all the grandees of Japan's remote past the Fujiwaras were careful to endorse Shinto as well as Buddhism, thus making doubly sure of blessings in the after-life as well as in this one. Kasuga Taisha is one of the most picturesque shrines in the country. The approach road is lined with 3000 lanterns donated by the faithful. All of them are lit two or three times a year, on 3 or 4 February and 14 and 15 August, making a fine spectacle.

Kasuga is also important architecturally. The style of building found inside its precincts, Kasuga-zukuri, is one of the basic shrine types and is found in the numerous other shrines established by the Fujiwara family around the country. The main shrine is composed of four separate, identical buildings lined up beside each other, one each for the four deities worshipped here, Takemikazuchi-no-mikoto and Futsu-nishi-no-mikoto, two gods famous for their exploits during the founding of the Japanese nation, and the divine ancestors of the Fujiwara family themselves, Ame-no-koyane-no-mikoto and his consort, Hime-gami. The design of the shrines is in essence very simple: a small gabled box one bay wide, with a pent roof over the steps at the front of the shrine which is attached to the gable. As at Izumo shrine, the characteristic *chigi* and *katsuogi* are merely decorative. The roofs, which curve steeply, are thatched.

In contrast to the melancholy emptiness of many great temples. Kasuga is full of life and activity. This is because the Shinto religion still plays such a vigorous role in everyday Japanese life. Visitors crowd through this shrine, some to have their weddings solemnized or their babies blessed, others to crave good luck in their examinations or some other undertaking, all in a state of great bustle and familial excitement,

PREVIOUS PAGES Shrines within shrines: in Japan Shinto shrines, sometimes very small, are erected wherever a numinous natural feature is considered to be worth marking. This small example, complete with *torii* entrance and box-like shrine structure, is within the precincts of the much grander Kasuga Shrine.

ABOVE Some of the 3,000 lanterns of the splendid Kasuga Shrine in Nara which were donated down the ages by believers to acquire merit. Two or three times a year they are all lit.

BELOW Detail of Kasuga Shrine's precincts, showing lanterns and a wooden bucket and dipper for visitors to wash their mouths and hands before entering. Traditionally the purification process necessary before entering a shrine could be very elaborate, involving practices such as the avoidance of all foods except those cooked over a ritually pure fire or total immersion in sea or river. Today purely symbolic purification with holy water is usually deemed sufficient.

while the shrine maidens in their multiple layers of silk kimono, sprays of paper wisteria bobbing from their foreheads, sit decorously behind wooden enclosures.

Down the hill from Kasuga and a short walk to the north stands Todaiji, 'Great Eastern Temple', the most awe-inspiring temple in the country. Its Buddha Hall, though slightly smaller than when originally constructed, is the largest wooden building in the world. When Nara was first laid out, Todaiji was given eight blocks of the city, an area four times larger than Kofukuji and equal to the imperial palace. Its construction, which began in 745, was the most intense and concentrated attempt by the Japanese to match and then surpass the achievements of the Chinese – the equivalent, perhaps, of Japan's pre-war development of the Mitsubishi Zero fighter plane, or the more recent exertions of Toyota and Nissan in beating the American car industry. They were no less successful in the eighth century than they have been in the twentieth: Todaiji's Buddha Hall (Daibutsuden) was bigger by far in its original form, at 290 by 170 T'ang feet (roughly the same as English feet), than the largest hall presently standing in the palace at Beijing, the T'ai-ho-tien. The ceremonial dedication of the temple in 752, attended by august figures from as far away as India, was the most magnificent international occasion in the nation's history, resounding proof that Japan had arrived on the world stage. But before the century was out, Nara had been abandoned as capital in favour of Heian (Kyoto). The power and political ambition of Todaiji's monks was too much of a threat.

Physically, at least, Todaiji still dominates Nara today. Seen from the road that leads from the station, the golden commas on the roof ridge of the Buddha Hall glint beckoningly. The approach road to the South Great Gate is the park's main street, cluttered with souvenir shops, crowded with tourists and the shabby deer that live off them. The gate itself, which dates from the twelfth century, is of stupendous size and is a foretaste of the majesty of what lies beyond – the Buddha Hall, behind its enclosing verandah wall. The vast, gloomy interior of the Hall is dominated by the seated golden image of the Great Buddha, the largest historic Buddha image in Japan. Much patched and repaired down the centuries, it lacks the serene beauty of the smaller Great Buddha in Kamakura, but its sheer size astonishes. The sect which built Todaiji has been moribund for centuries, but this image still has a magnetic appeal. At the base of one of the pillars on the right side of the hall is a hole which is said to be exactly the same size as the image's nostrils, and often parents can be seen attempting to thrust their reluctant small children through it, in the belief that it will bring them good luck. Stalls set up inside the hall do a thriving trade in telephone cards bearing the Buddha's likeness, fortune-telling papers and various other pious knick-knacks.

Todaiji has had a tempestuous history. Although the Buddha Hall's size has enabled it to sit out typhoons which destroyed smaller temples and other buildings, including the South Great Gate, it is the same factor – its scale – coupled with the ambition of its priests that has twice brought about its destruction. The first occasion was during the bitter wars between the Taira and Minamoto clans which brought the Heian period to an end in the twelfth century. The monks took the side of Minamoto, whereupon the Taira burned the whole complex to the ground and slaughtered many of the monks. The two mammoth seven-storey pagodas which until then had flanked the Buddha Hall at the front were lost, and were never to be rebuilt. This disaster took place in 1180, but soon afterwards the Minamoto defeated the Taira for good, and one of the first things they did was to rebuild the temple. The man appointed for the job was a monk called Chogen, one of the last great Japanese pilgrims to China; a wooden statue of him is to be found in the Shunjo-do, to the right of the Buddha Hall. For reasons which scholars still argue over, and which may simply have been due to the arrival of a particular team of craftsmen from China at the right moment, Chogen chose to have both the South Great Gate and the Buddha Hall rebuilt in a style which had never been seen in Japan before, and which was rarely to be seen again.

This was the *Tenjikuyo* or 'Indian style', though its relation to anything Indian is at best remote. It probably originated in the south of China, though even this cannot be said with certainty as no buildings from the Sung period in this manner survive. The most distinctive feature is a radically different approach to the bracketing which supports the eaves. The classical form of bracketing, seen in mature form at Toshodaiji, achieves both strength and grace by sprouting out in two dimensions from the capital at the top of each column. In the reconstruction of Todaiji, by contrast, the columns do not terminate in capitals but rise all the way to the roof – a design feature, incidentally,

which required the use of stupendously tall trees which were only to be found deep in the mountains. The brackets notch directly into the columns and project straight out, in one dimension only, rising up in steeply angled upward steps, each arm ending in a bearing-block which cradles the arm above. There is something uncouth as well as structurally unsatisfactory about the design, the uncouth impression reinforced by the almost complete absence from the building of the ornamental graces familiar in an earlier age. But used on the scale necessary in a building of this size, there is an immense power in the insistent, single-minded upward drive, with something about it of the awesome verticality of Gothic architecture.

Robbed of its pagodas but endowed with a new type of splendour, this was how Todaiji stood for the next four centuries. But during the anarchic period that preceded the rise of the Tokugawa shoguns in the mid-sixteenth century, the Buddha Hall was once again destroyed, and what remained of the Buddha image was left out in the open for a century. At the start of the eighteenth century, however, and as an advertisement for the stability and prosperity which the Tokugawa regime had brought, the Hall was reconstructed a second time. It was only partial, and lacked the finesse of Chogen's work; the façade was spoiled by the insertion of a device very popular in the Tokugawa period, a decorative curved hood, over the entrance, between the two roofs. The scale was still tremendous, however, the Buddha was back indoors and Nara had regained its most impressive monument.

Todaiji's completion in 752 was the consummate achievement of the Nara period. Just thirty-two years later the Emperor Kammu moved his court again, to Nagaoka, 35 kilometres to the north, to distance himself from Nara's unruly priests. Ten years after that, fearing that Nagaoka had become infested by evil spirits, he moved once again, this time to Kyoto, a little further north. And this time the capital stayed put: the court was not to move again for over a thousand years. The history of what was to become Japan's most celebrated city of culture and religion had begun.

In a few years Nara sank back into the status of a small provincial town, adorned with bizarrely disproportionate monuments, which is how it remains to this day.

3   Kyoto

Kinkakuji, Kyoto's glorious Temple of the Golden Pavilion, which was rebuilt in 1955 after its destruction by arson. The ground floor, designed in the palace style, is called *Hosuiin*, the Chamber of Dharma Waters; the first floor, which contains an image of Kannon, is called *Choonkaku*, the Tower of the Sound of Waves; and the second floor, *Kukyocho* or the Cupola of the Ultimate, houses an Amida triad and twenty-five bodhisattva images. The latticed, cusped windows of the second floor are typical of Zen temple architecture.

Any city with over a thousand years of history is bound to be a tangle of stories and traditions, achievements and disasters, through which it is hard or impossible to trace the original reality. This is both more and less true of Kyoto than of other great cities of comparable age. Less true because the original plan of the city as laid out at the end of the eighth century by Emperor Kammu's architects, though modified in many important respects, is still the basic shape of the city today. More true because until the age of ferroconcrete Kyoto's buildings were always made of wood, and consequently very vulnerable to the attrition of war and natural disaster. Very little indeed survives of Kyoto's original buildings – though a great deal survives from later periods.

Kyoto today is an extraordinary city. It can be a great disappointment for those seeing it for the first time. Kyoto the Beautiful, the tag attached by the tourist authorities, seems a sick joke to many making their first forays into the place. Because of its fantastic cultural heritage it was spared the bombings that destroyed most Japanese cities at the end of the Pacific War. But since then the Japanese have themselves done quite as good a job of destroying the city's ancient atmosphere. In many ways Kyoto is just another large, prosperous, thoroughly modernized and thoroughly mediocre Japanese city, its permanently congested main roads lined with large, nondescript buildings lacking any architectural merit whatever.

Yet Kyoto is also much more than this. It takes a little time and perseverance to discover the vast treasury of beauty and antiquity that the city hoards. This is pre-eminently a Buddhist city: every important sect which flourished in Japan after the achievements of Nara has a major temple or monastery in the city or on its outskirts. And most of these are far more than just ancient monuments: they are still vital centres of pilgrimage or meditation. Those that are not lively in this way, because in religious terms they never amounted to more than toys of the rich and powerful, are none the less magnificently preserved. Kinkakuji, the famous Temple of the Golden Pavilion, was recently treated to another coat of gold leaf, and the exquisite Ginkakuji, the Silver Pavilion on the other side of the city, can never have looked more beautiful than it does now. These are some of the compensations of affluence.

The plan adopted for Kyoto was similar to that of Nara, though

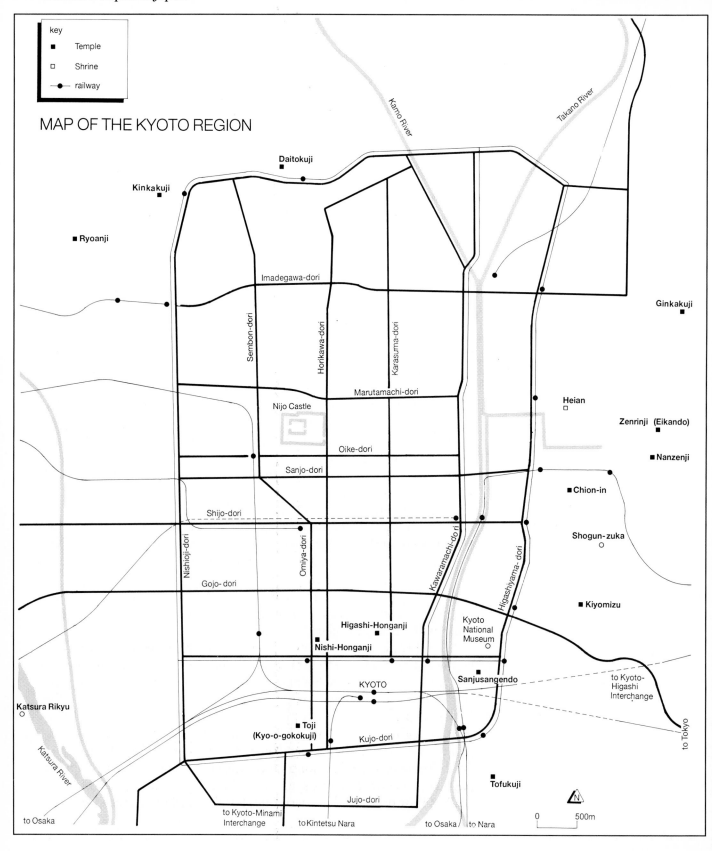

Wooden Temples of Japan

key

■ Temple

□ Shrine

●— railway

MAP OF THE KYOTO REGION

Daitokuji

Kinkakuji

Ryoanji

Kamo River

Takano River

Imadegawa-dori

Ginkakuji

Sembon-dori

Horikawa-dori

Karasuma-dori

Marutamachi-dori

Heian

Zenrinji (Eikando)

Nijo Castle

Oike-dori

Nanzenji

Sanjo-dori

Chion-in

Shijo-dori

Shogun-zuka

Nishioji-dori

Omiya-dori

Kawaramachi-dori

Higashiyama-dori

Kiyomizu

Gojo-dori

Higashi-Honganji

Kyoto National Museum

Nishi-Honganji

KYOTO

Sanjusangendo

to Kyoto-Higashi Interchange

Katsura Rikyu

Toji (Kyo-o-gokokuji)

Kujo-dori

to Tokyo

Katsura River

Tofukuji

N

Jujo-dori

0   500m

to Osaka

to Kyoto-Minami Interchange

to Kintetsu Nara

to Osaka / to Nara

slightly larger. Like all the capitals designed under the influence of the T'ang dynasty, it was rigidly schematic, a grid divided by nine streets running from east to west, from Ichijo, First Street, in the north, to Kujo, Ninth Street, in the south. Several of the streets in the city today correspond exactly to these east–west divisions – and in general the old grid has been well enough preserved to make Kyoto almost as easy to negotiate as Manhattan, and easier by far than, say, Tokyo. Suzaku Oji, however, has gone. This vast, very Chinese boulevard, 82 metres wide and lined with willows, divided the city in two, with the left half on the east and the right half on the west, which corresponded to the way the country was divided administratively, with responsibility split between the ministers of the left and right. The imperial palace, in the extreme north and theoretically right in the middle (though actually with slightly more of it in the east, the direction of which the Japanese were privately fondest), occupied a vast area in the city as first constituted – one-fifth of the whole. Never again, Emperor Kammu must have vowed, would emperors allow themselves to be bullied by the priests. In the long run he was wrong.

The city was about five kilometres from north to south and four and a half from east to west. The north–south measurement still defines pretty accurately the city centre, but not long after its foundation it was learned that the western half was awkwardly marshy. An eastward drift commenced until, as today, important parts of the city were located on the far side of the Kamo River, whose course, ironically, had been specially altered at the time of the city's foundation to avoid just such an eventuality. In the modern city the awesome Suzaku Oji has shrunk to the more congenially Japanese dimensions of Sembon Dori, not much wider than any other Japanese high street.

This, then, is the city centre – but, with about three exceptions, the temples which most repay a visit are outside it. There are several reasons for this. When Heian-kyo, Kyoto's original name, was first established, the emperor was so fearful of the political ambition of the Buddhist priesthood that he permitted the construction of only two temples within the city limits, both in the extreme south, as far from the palace as possible. These were Toji and Saiji, literally East Temple and West Temple. Saiji has long since vanished. Toji remains, and its pagoda is one of the city's symbols and the highest in Japan. The veto on Buddhist power did not last long, but the newly introduced esoteric

Rigorously disciplined trees by the main building of Zuishin-in temple, erected in the early eleventh century by a member of the powerful Fujiwara family as a votive prayer for the soul of his mother.

sects, Tendai and Shingon, which reasserted it a couple of centuries later, had a different conception of where the temple belonged: not in the heart of the metropolis but in the heart of the mountains, where the severity of the living conditions and the proximity to nature provided a more sympathetic environment for the attainment of insight. The Zen sects which entered Japan later also valued natural beauty and tranquillity, and located themselves on the city's mountainous fringes. Only the populist sects which flourished at the same time as Zen, in the anarchy of the thirteenth century and later, notably the Jodo Shin sect, rediscovered a place for Buddhism in the heart of the city, and its temples are there still.

The pleasures of exploring Kyoto are the pleasures of serendipity – of stumbling on this little rock garden, that neighbourhood shrine with its swings and children, a perfectly preserved row of old town houses or a tumbledown temple. But it may be useful to sketch in the particular areas of historical interest that the city's temples encompass. The one significant temple whose foundation just predates the establishment of the city is Kiyomizu-dera, over to the east, and it is also one of the most popular and picturesque, enjoying splendid views from its famous *butai* or scaffold. Toji is the principal temple to survive from the Heian period, though it still feels just as peripheral as Emperor Kammu intended and rather melancholy in mood as a consequence, but it possesses some fabulous statuary. The most important temples of the Tendai and Shingon sects, those semi-magical denominations whose fascination with mandalas, mystical words and agonizing ascetic practices links them closely with the Buddhism of Tibet, are way outside the city, on Mts Hiei and Koya respectively. Several of Kyoto's most exquisite temples are the work of the aristocratic families which dominated the city at different periods, the Fujiwara and later the Ashikaga. The Fujiwara's memorial is Byodo-in, the Ashikaga's Kinkakuji and Ginkakuji. Their mood of refinement marks them out from all other temples of all other eras, because these were not temples at all as traditionally understood, but the extravagant religious follies of their wealthy patrons.

The Zen sect made its mark on the city in between the eclipse of the Fujiwara and the ascendancy of the Ashikaga, in the thirteenth century. The training of monks was central to Zen and the great monasteries of Daitokuji and Nanzenji are still flourishing. Of the two, Daitokuji is perhaps the more impressive. Within its expansive grounds it contains so much that is central to the Buddhist heritage in Japan: both the solemn, monumental, unpainted, symmetrically arranged halls of the temple proper with their portentous bracketing, their powerful, immemorial forms; and the numerous small sub-temples and hermitages dotted around them, innocent of all continental pomposity, each with its particular beauties of garden or tea-room.

Lastly there are the great centres of the new, popular Buddhism of the Jodo Shin sect, Nishi-Honganji and Higashi-Honganji. The original sect split centuries ago, and the two factions have remained firmly opposed ever since. Their great temples are remarkably similar, however, and remarkably different from all the others, dominated by their vast founder's halls. Hulkingly impressive, they make up in popularity with their adherents for what they lack in grace.

I have made no mention of shrines, and indeed Kyoto is far more of a Buddhist than a Shinto city. None of the dozens of little Shinto shrines around the city has anything approaching the significance of its temples. The only exception, Heian Jingu, is an equivocal one because it is of no age at all, and it is not even really a shrine like any other in the country. It is a half-size replica of the Daigoku-den, the Hall of State, of Emperor Kammu as it existed in Kyoto's first incarnation, and it enshrines the spirit of that founding father. It was built in the late nineteenth century to mark the 1100th anniversary of the foundation of Heian-kyo, and was intended as an awe-inspiring symbol of the imperial family's continuity, to bolster the prestige of State Shinto, the artificial codification of the native religion by which the nation's new, modern rulers hoped to galvanize the patriotic feelings of the people. They were successful, of course, as Pearl Harbor and Hiroshima bear witness – all of which rather takes the shine off Heian Jingu's gleaming, tangerine-coloured walls and bright green roofs, at least for the foreign visitor with a sense of history. But its blinding expanses of white gravel are not a popular focus of pilgrimage even for Japanese. It is an obligatory coach stop rather than the sort of place people flock to by choice.

Kiyomizudera

Kiyomizudera, the complex perched on a steep hill to the east of the city centre, is one of the most famous landmarks in Japan. The temple's

Hon-do is elevated on a great scaffold, and the temple itself, by virtue of both its age and its fabulous location, transcends the factional bickering that marks many other places in the city: it belongs not just to one sect, nor just to Kyoto, but to the whole nation. The dizzying view from the temple has become proverbial: to throw oneself from the scaffold of Kiyomizu means to launch into the unknown.

The legend goes that a young novice called Enchin dreamed of seeing a golden stream flowing into the Todogawa River, and on waking went in search of it. When he found it and followed it to its source he discovered an old man sitting under a tree, waiting for him. The old man said, 'I have been here for the last two hundred years, waiting for you to relieve me'. He added that this spot was suitable for the erection of a hermitage, and that the great log lying close by would make ideal raw material for an image of Kannon. At this the old man disappeared. Intuiting that the old man had been Kannon himself in disguise, Enchin resolved to carve the image as instructed, but found his strength insufficient, and for twenty years gazed forlornly at the log, wondering what to do next. At this point a warrior named Saka-no-ue Tamuramaro happened by in pursuit of a stag. Enchin unburdened himself, and 'Top-of-the-hill' Tamuramaro was so moved by the novice's devotion that he dismantled his own house and had it rebuilt by the side of the waterfall to house the image Enchin had by this time finally completed. The last part of the legend enters the realm of fact, for Top-of-the-hill was a historical figure whose life overlapped Kyoto's foundation; and to this day the Hon-do, much the largest and most impressive building in the complex, and the one which stands on the site of the original Tamura-do, looks more like a great house than any conventional temple building.

That may of course be chance: Kiyomizu has burned down six times since its foundation, the last time being in 1629, after which it was rebuilt again in 1633. None the less, it is certainly one of the strangest and most distinctive Buddhist structures in Japan. Supported by the huge scaffold which has its feet on the valley floor, it is covered by an immense, homely shingle roof, like an archaic farm house. Smaller pent *irimoya* roofs project from the corners, covering the projections from the scaffold and giving an effect reminiscent of the stage of a Noh theatre. Like the Tendai temples of Mt Hiei, the temple's plan is powerfully modified by the mountainous setting. In Kiyomizu's case the

The huge wooden *butai* or scaffold which supports the Main Hall of Kiyomizudera, one of Kyoto's most ancient and popular temples. The scaffold is a byword for vertigo in Japan. Photo © Takeji Iwamiya.

single axis along which the buildings are strung runs from west to east: the ascent from the city is up steep Kiyomizu Zaka (hill), nicknamed Teapot Lane on account of the pottery shops which line it, then passes through the Sai Mon, West Gate, of the Momoyama period, past the three-storey pagoda (also rebuilt 1633), the original founder's hall and other structures, before culminating in the mighty Hon-do. The view over the city to the south is a more than adequate reward for the effort of the ascent.

To go back to the legend: the reason Top-of-the-hill Tamuramaro came across the benighted Enchin was because he was deer-hunting, and he was deer-hunting because his wife was pregnant and deerskin was considered the ideal talisman for easy childbirth. According to one version of the story, it was just as he killed the deer that he bumped into Enchin, who at once gave him a lecture on the wrongness of killing animals. The nobleman penitently buried the deer he had killed, and his wife had an easy childbirth all the same – in reward, no doubt, for her husband's piety. Prayers for trouble-free delivery have been said here ever since. The particular focus of such prayers is Taian-ji, 'Gentle Delivery Temple', a sub-temple at the complex's south-eastern edge, comprising a main hall with an image of Koyasu ('Easy Child') Kannon which is more than 1200 years old, and a small pagoda.

Even leaving aside his role in the foundation of Kiyomizu, Tamuramaro is an interesting figure. He was the first Japanese military man to be accorded the title *sei-tai-shogun*, or shogun for short, which means 'barbarian-subduing generalissimo', and sent to the far north to do just that to the unruly aborigines. His tomb is found directly behind Kiyomizu, and it is called *shogun-zuka*. A groaning sound is said to issue from it whenever Kyoto is in danger.

Because of its early foundation, Kiyomizu rather stands apart from the battle of the sects which is in part the history of Kyoto as a religious centre. It belongs to the long-moribund Hosso sect, to which also belong Kofukuji, Yakushiji and Horyuji, all in Nara, but no other temples in Kyoto. Like the Nanendo sub-temple of Kofukuji, Kiyomizu is on the Thirty-three Temple pilgrimage route. Which is one more reason, in addition to the hopes of easy childbirth, the picturesque legends, the worldwide fame and the great views, why Kiyomizu is always full of people.

Toji and Saiji

Toji and Saiji, East Temple and West Temple, were *of* Kyoto the capital as Kiyomizu never was. Their intended relation to the imperial house was expressed by the geographical position, far to the south, and by their proper names. Toji, built in 796, was formally called Kyogokuji, 'Protecting-the-country temple'. It stood at the city's boundary like the fearsome guardian statues found at the entrance gates of the temples themselves.

Saiji soon disappeared altogether and Toji might have suffered the same fate. But in 823 it gained a new lease of life when it was entrusted to one of the most famous Buddhist teachers in Japanese history, Kukai, or to give him the posthumous name by which he is universally known in Japan, Kobo Daishi. Kukai's principal achievement was in bringing the new Shingon sect to Japan from China. As a result, Toji became the capital's first Shingon temple, replete with that sect's paraphernalia of images and mandalas. But Kukai was far more than just an enterprising cleric. His status in Japan is semi-legendary: he is credited with inventing *hiragana*, one of the two Japanese syllabaries, with singlehandedly excavating great tunnels, and many other heroic achievements besides.

The Shingon sect proved quite as politically meddlesome as its predecessors at Nara. It asserted that it was both the heart of Buddha and the soul of the state. Emperor Kammu had by this time passed away, however, and his heir, Saga, was receptive to the sect's message. It was probably made more palatable by Kukai's promise to build his headquarters in the heart of the mountains, which he duly did, though he also built a more modest Shingon centre within the imperial court.

In form Toji hearkens back to the simplicity of Shittenoji in Osaka, the first temple in the country, in that the principal buildings are simply strung out on a single axis from the South Great Gate. The single massive pagoda stands to the east. It took the best part of a century to build it, and it is the tallest in the country. The temple has been somewhat carelessly adapted to modern conditions, its spaces broken up by fences to prevent people who have not paid the entrance fee from getting at the main buildings, the pretty garden with a pond near the pagoda defiled by ugly little tin benches sponsored by Coca-Cola, the pagoda itself mutilated in the name of fire prevention. Once inside the buildings, however, and the Kodo, Lecture Hall, in particular, all such imperfections are forgotten. Toji is a splendid museum of Heian period art: the host of Buddhas, Bodhisattvas and heavenly kings stand out in the gloom, their patinas of old gold glinting faintly, their capacity to evoke awe and devotion so much more readily understood here than behind glass or under the bright lights of a conventional museum.

At the centre is Buddha Dainichi surrounded by the four Kongo-kai Buddhas, Buddhas of the Diamond World, representing his diamond-hard wisdom. To their right are five Bodhisattvas, the saints peculiar to the Mahayana school of Buddhism (the branch which flourished in China and Japan) who declined complete Buddha-hood so they could work in the world to bring all sentient beings to enlightenment. To their left are the Five Wrathful Gods whose pious aim was the same as that of the Bodhisattvas, but whose means was terror. Guarding the whole group at the corners are the Shitenno, the Four Heavenly Kings. The whole complex arrangement reflects the intricate Buddhist cosmogony by which the universe was divided into zones, each ruled by a different Buddha or Bodhisattva. Like the stained glass of a medieval church, the statues brought home the doctrines, the terrors and promises of the religion to the many devotees for whom the archaic words of the sacred texts were beyond comprehension.

Other images in Toji's grounds include one of Bishamon, who is one of the Four Heavenly Kings, in the Shoku-do (Refectory), and the oldest surviving statue of Kukai himself, sculpted in 1233, which stands in the Taishi-do Hall, erected on the site of the priest's living quarters. Kukai is also remembered in the markets held in the temple grounds on the twenty-first of each month, the anniversary of his death.

Kukai's great peer as a promulgator of esoteric Buddhism was the priest Saicho who founded the Tendai sect. Saicho's monument is the great complex of temples to the north-east of the city called Enryaku-ji. While Toji and Saiji were posted as guardians on the south of the city, the direction from which the Japanese traditionally have the greatest fear of evil is the north-east. This is the location of the *Kimon,* the 'devil's gate' in traditional city design. Even before Heian-kyo was established a cluster of huts was built on Mt Hiei, north-east of where the city was to be, with the idea of repelling evil. Saicho was the man who put them there. The sect he founded, given authority by the scriptures he brought back from China in 805 after a stay of less than a

ABOVE Side view of Byodo-in's
Phoenix Hall, with the pool in
front. The hall was the most
famous and splendid example of
the fashion among court nobles
towards the end of the Heian
period for building private buddha
halls, *jibutsudo*, on the grounds of
their residences, to encourage pious
thoughts.

BELOW Detail of the roof at the
Phoenix Hall of Byodo-in, at Uji,
south-east of Kyoto. These
apparently flimsy members have
withstood centuries of neglect since
the hall was built in 1053.

year, grew to be one of the most potent religious sects in the country; it
also grew, ironically enough, into one of the most formidable political
forces in the capital. Far from guarding against problems originating in
the north-east, it became the main source of them.

Time after time the militant, fully armed monks marched down on
the capital to bully rival sects or to endorse or oppose the actions of the
emperor. So powerful did they become that they invariably got their
way. So effectively did they amass power and wealth that at the height
of their prosperity they had more than 3000 temple buildings sprawled
across the mountains. Finally, however, the provocation they represented proved too much. The first of the three generals who brought
about the unification of the country, Oda Nobunaga, attacked the
monastery in 1571, burned all the buildings and massacred the priests.
A miniature pagoda in the woods behind the present temple's Shaka-do
(Buddha Hall), just 1.5 metres high, is the only structure of the Heian
period which survived.

The temple complex was rebuilt under Nobunaga's successor,
Hideyoshi, but only attained a fraction of its former size – some 125
buildings. That is roughly the number that exists today, dotted across
the mountainside, buried among the trees, their air of remoteness from
the city as strong as ever. The views from the mountain-top across Lake
Biwa to the foothills of the Japan Alps in the east are exhilarating.

The Phoenix Hall of Byodo-in

About as far to the south-east of Kyoto as Mt Hiei is to the north-east
stands the most beautiful and famous architectural relic of the Heian
period, the Phoenix Hall of Byodo-in, the Temple of Equality. This is
also the most impressive memorial to the period of Japanese history
when one family, the Fujiwaras, by diligently intermarrying with the
imperial family generation after generation, attained something close to
absolute power; the point, just before the start of its slow collapse,
when the civilisation of the Heian period attained its peak of elegant
accomplishment.

The Phoenix Hall is a symbol of all these things. Fujiwara Michinaga,
born in 966, was the most famous and successful of his whole clan.
Four of his daughters married men who became emperors, while the
fifth married a crown prince. All eight emperors of the eleventh century
were the husbands or sons of these women. Michinaga's power was

unassailable, so he was free to spread his wealth around as elegantly and conspicuously as he liked. His favourite way of doing this was to build great temples – not centres of popular Buddhism, but extravagant follies which were as much imitations of heaven as places of worship. It was a very particular vision of heaven which they enshrined. The school of Buddhism which held the imperial court in its spell during Heian was the cult of Amida, Lord of the Western Paradise, and Michinaga's private temples were depictions of that paradise. The long-vanished temple of Hojoji, for example, is described in the contemporary *Eiga Monogatari* as having trees with leaves of pearl, gold, amber and lapis, a pool of gold and jade, columns with bases of ivory, roof ridges of red gold, gilded doors and platforms of crystal.

The Phoenix Hall is very much in the same spirit, but it is not in fact Michinaga's work. He built a villa on this site, but it was Yorimichi, his eldest son, who converted it into a temple. This included the Phoenix Hall, which was completed in 1053. Yorimichi also became the most powerful man in the country, marrying off two of his daughters to future emperors, but his was to be the last blaze of the glory of the Fujiwaras. He retired to Uji (where Byodo-in is located) in 1067, living there until his death seven years later. Meanwhile one of the very few truly dynamic emperors in Japanese history succeeded briefly in seizing the reins of power, and the eleventh century was to see the snuffing-out of all remaining Fujiwara influence and the end of the Heian period with which the family was so closely identified. Byodo-in, lacking institutional support, declined with the family. A great fire in 1483 consumed the whole complex except the Phoenix Hall, which was probably protected by its pool. Its neglect continued until the twentieth century and it was only restored to its original splendour between 1950 and 1957, at a cost of 70 million yen.

In China, Amida's heaven had naturally enough been described in terms of what was regarded then as the closest possible equivalent on earth, the Chinese imperial park – descendants of which are to be found still in Beijing and Seoul. It was this model which was imitated by Amida's aristocratic devotees in Japan.

The most striking feature of all such 'paradises', and the one which marks them off from the temples of all other sects, is the central pool, interposed between the south gate and the main building. It is one of the magical features of Byodo-in. The other is the form of the hall itself.

One of the twin phoenixes on the roof of Byodo-in's Phoenix Hall – although the name of the hall derives as much from the shape of the buildings, with its wing-like corridors to the side and even a tail-like appendage to the rear, as from the birds perched above it.

The Phoenix Hall's celebrated gilt statue of Amida Buddha, with an opulent gilt mandorla behind it and an elaborate canopy above. Amida worship was part of the Pure Land (*Jodo*) school of Buddhism, originally linked to the esoteric Tendai sect, whose simple prescriptions for eternal life in the Pure Land appealed to aristocrats as well as commoners during the Heian period.

Like the Heian Hall of State, this was inspired by the Chinese T'ang palaces which were the centerpiece of the Chinese Amida gardens. This is revealed most clearly in the small corner pavilions, accommodated at the point where the corridors projecting from the hall turn the corner to face the pond and then stop short. These pavilions have no function – they are not high enough for a man to stand in – but they echo the more developed side corridors found in the (now vanished) temples of the same date whose grounds were more generous. And their visual function is plain: they are the wings of the phoenix, as the hall is the head. The profusion of gently inclined, suavely upswinging roofs gives to the whole form an effervescent lightness which is compounded by the reflection in the pool. It really does float.

Almost as celebrated as the Phoenix Hall itself is the image of Amida it contains. This is by Jocho, whose famous work is also seen in Nara's Kofukuji. This Amida is noted for the modesty and humanity of its realism: Amida is one of us, of humbly human proportions – it just happens that, with his flat, protruding knees, his fingers resting together, his eyes downturned, his mouth neither open nor shut, he is in a perfectly communicated state of grace.

Uji, the place where the Phoenix Hall stands, was not picked by the Fujiwaras at random. With its clean air and pretty river, it was the perfect spot for such bucolic Heian pastimes as firefly hunting and cormorant fishing, in which trained cormorants on leashes catch and then deliver the fish to revellers in boats. The latter sport is still enjoyed in the summer, but fireflies are not so easy to come by. The cormorant fishing takes place every night between 11 June and 31 August except on nights of a full moon, or when there have been heavy rains.

The rise of the warriors and the coming of Zen

As the power of both the imperial family and the Fujiwaras waned through the latter half of the eleventh century, they came to depend more and more on the vigour of warrior clans from the provinces to protect them. Two clans in particular competed for primacy: the Taira (also called Heike) and the Minamoto. Their struggle and its resolution were in a short space to bring the Heian period to an end. The rise of its warriors, the samurai, is one of the turning-points in Japanese history. It brought with it a new mental toughness, the code of samurai ethics, the eclipse (though not the extinction) of the imperial house, the opening up and civilizing of eastern Japan, and the introduction of the last new sects of Buddhism from the continent which were to dig roots and really flourish in the country. It was the sort of massive shake-up, comparable to the rise of the Tokugawa in the sixteenth century and the restoration of the emperor in 1868, which seems to be the closest Japan ever comes to a revolution.

One of Kyoto's most popular attractions for visitors is a sort of halfway house between the Heian emperors and the new period which was in the making. This is Sanjusangendo Temple, a little way south of Kyoto National Museum, near the city centre. *Sanjusangen* means 'thirty-three bays', referring to the enormous length of the temple's main hall. The bays accommodate the temple's collection of 1001 figures of Kannon, Goddess of Mercy, and considering the career of the temple's sponsor, Emperor Goshirakawa, it is not surprising that he should have felt so much in need of protection. Goshirakawa was thrust on to the throne in 1156 on the death in adolescence of his predecessor, whereupon he immediately found himself at the centre of a war between the rival warrior clans. The Taira, who had taken his side, won it, but three years later a dissident member of the faction, Yoshitomo, who was in fact a turncoat Minamoto, burned down the emperor's palace in an attempt to take him prisoner, killing many of his attendants. Kiyomori, head of the Taira clan, rushed back to the emperor's aid. Yoshitomo was beheaded, and for a few years throne and samurai enjoyed an uneasy détente. But the people of Kyoto knew it could not last. Such was the cruelty of the wars, they were convinced that they were now living in hell, and would henceforth be ruled by devils.

The nervous extravagance of Sanjusangendo reflects this mood. As the emperor's temporal power was clearly on the decline, there was nothing left but to resort to magic. Besides being the number of the temple's bays, thirty-three is also the number of shapes that Kannon can assume on her errands of mercy. The central image is of Kannon with 1000 hands, and was the work of a sculptor called Tankei. It was carved in 1254, and is a national treasure. As well as this overpowering abundance of the embodiments of Mercy, the temple also houses twenty-eight attendant guardians and other protective figures such as the God of Thunder and the God of Wind. While Emperor Goshirakawa was the begetter of the temple, he entrusted its construction to his warrior saviour Kiyomori, and these guardian figures represent the role which Kiyomori and his soldiers chose to allot themselves in the cosmic scheme of things. With its crowds of sacred bully-boys, anything further from the serenity of the Phoenix Hall is hard to imagine.

As it turned out, a bare twenty years were to pass before the destruction of this fragile status quo. All the gods in the universe were not enough to save the Taira, who were finally wiped out at the sea battle of Dannoura in 1185. The victor was the Minamoto chieftain Yoritomo, and his most dramatic decision in his triumph was to move his headquarters — and with it the *de facto* capital of the country — hundreds of kilometres to the north-east, to the fishing village of Kamakura, some sixty kilometres south of Tokyo. It was there that the nation's seat of government remained for more than a century. Despite its loss? of temporal power, Koyoto did not disappear from the picture. The emperors and the aristocracy remained with their estates, their dignity, their own imaginative and spiritual world, and what was left of their wealth. And bit by bit their vices of indolence and pride infected the soldiers who had supplanted them.

The establishment of a new order allowed winds of change to blow through the institutions of late Heian, and the strongest and freshest of these was the new sect of Buddhism that arrived from the continent, the Zen sect (Ch'an in Chinese). Zen appealed to Japan's new military rulers for much the same reasons that it has made such a strong impact in the West during the past fifty years. In contrast to the fantastic esoteric complexities of the Tendai and Shingon sects, Zen marked a return to the most basic yet most difficult essential of the religion: the practice of meditation.

To the surprise of many Western enthusiasts, Japanese Zen monasteries have their share of images of Kannon, Amida and so on, as well as Shakyamuni, the historical Buddha. The monks chant sutras as do those of other sects. But the heart of the Zen practice is silent meditation, as it was the heart of the practice of Shakyamuni himself. And the goal of the meditation, like Shakyamuni's, though stressed in varying degrees by the different schools of Zen, is the attainment of enlightenment through direct experience of the truth of Buddhism, that the material world and everything in it is illusory.

This was a return to the basics of Buddhism with a vengeance. The rigour of the teaching involved a comparable rigour in the life of the

One of the main structures at Nanzenji, illustrating the powerful and complicated bracketing system preferred by the Zen sect's architects to keep their roofs up. The cusped arches of the windows on the ground floor, another typical Zen feature, are clearly visible.

monks. It put a new stress on the characters of the Zen masters, the abbots who founded, led and inspired the new communities of monks. No longer was it enough to recite endlessly and mechanically certain magical syllables to attain salvation, nor was it sufficient to endure fixed and formulated hardships. The hours of meditation were punctuated by interviews with the master who would probe the acolyte's mental state, attempting by words or actions to smash the illusions that separated him from enlightenment. In the Rinzai school, one of the two main schools into which Zen divided, stress came to be laid on the famous *koan*, impossible riddles on which the young monks had to brood. The first koan for novices was the one called Joshu's Dog, which goes as follows:

A monk asked Zen Master Joshu, 'Master, does a dog have Buddha nature?'

Joshu answered 'Mu!'

'Mu' is not a word in its own right but a prefix meaning 'not' or 'un-', so it seems that Joshu is saying 'No'. This cannot be, however, for Buddhism teaches that all sentient beings, from kings to cockroaches, have Buddha nature. So what does Joshu mean by this negating syllable? That is the impossible problem. The young monks focus on it for years if necessary, each 'solution' he brings to the master being treated with contempt – until one day, in the intensity of his frustration, the conceptual dam breaks and he is overwhelmed by an instant of direct, intuitive understanding which the master, who would not have got where he is without having achieved a similar breakthrough himself, recognizes at once.

This was the bracing if rather terrifyingly vertiginous new spiritual world that the missionaries from China brought, and they endeared themselves at once to the hard, rough-hewn men of the new regime. It was at Kamakura that the first of the new monasteries were established. But before long Zen turned up in Kyoto, too, and several of the most splendid Zen temples are to be found here.

Nanzenji

As well as a new/old form of practice and a new interpretation of Buddhism, the Zen teachers brought a new architecture, though like the sect itself, it was in many ways a return to basics. It was named *karayo*, 'Chinese-style'. All the experimentation with the layout of temple

ABOVE Garden and roofs at Nanzenji, illustrating the concept of 'borrowed scenery'. The forested mountain in the background is far away, but such remote features were taken into account by the designers of gardens and used to give their miniature creations depth and grandeur.

BELOW View of Nanzenji's Sanmon Gate from the front. It is also called *Tenka-no-Ryumon*, 'World Famous Dragon Gate', and is reputed to be one of the three biggest gates in Japan. First built in 1296, it was destroyed by fire in 1447 and reconstructed in 1626.

buildings of the past centuries was jettisoned. Zen restored the simplicity of foundation found at Shittenoji: an entrance in the south, wherever possible, and a single axis leading from there through, successively, the Sammon (Triple Gate), the Butsuden or Buddha Hall and the Hatto or Dharma Hall. The evidence that remains suggests that the imitation here of Chinese models was as close and faithful as could be achieved, though the point cannot be proved as none of the Chinese originals survives.

One of the first to be built in Kyoto was the magnificent Nanzenji, north-east of the city centre, hard by the eastern hills. Its establishment at the end of the thirteenth century, a hundred years after the advent of the Kamakura shogunate and half a century after the building of the first Zen temples in Kamakura, indicates that already the boot of cultural hegemony had transferred to the warrior's foot, for the founder of Nanzenji was not a samurai but an ex-emperor called Kameyama. Zen was becoming the new orthodoxy. Legend has it that Kameyama himself lugged some of the material for the temple's main hall, the Nanzen-in. The grounds contain a statue of him, dressed as a priest.

Nanzenji occupies the southern reach of that part of north-east Kyoto where the 'Philosopher's Path' meanders north along a pretty brook to the perfection of the Silver Pavilion. Vegetarian food was the rule in Zen monasteries, and the modern legacy of that custom is to be found in the numerous restaurants on the approach to Nanzenji which serve *yudofu*, 'hot water tofu' as it translates literally and unappetizingly, tastier than it sounds and very warming in winter.

Dominating the entrance to the monastery grounds is the Triple Gate, one of the architectural novelties which Zen introduced. Like many Zen temple buildings around the country, this is in fact an Edo period reconstruction, but just as the original buildings were faithful to the Chinese model, so the reconstructions are believed to be fairly close replicas of the originals. The novelty here is not just the three openings but the upper storey of the imposing structure, reached by a detached stair-house at either end. Upstairs are a number of statues including a seated Buddha and images of the great shogun Ieyasu, sponsor of the structure's rebuilding in the seventeenth century. The ceiling is decorated with paintings of phoenixes and angels.

The characteristic simplicity of Nanzenji's plan, leading up to the Main Hall, a modern structure replacing the one that burned down in

ABOVE Arches of the aqueduct to the east of Nanzenji, whose purpose is to feed the waterfall in one of Nanzenji's sub-temples. By such difficult means are some of Japan's 'natural' effects contrived.

BELOW AND BELOW RIGHT On the fringes of Kyoto, where the Zen sect chose to build its temples, trees and mountains give a sensual richness to the landscape, and a ravishing variety of tints in autumn. These scenes are at Nanzenji.

ABOVE Seated Buddha on the
upper floor of the Sanmon Gate at
Nanzenji, surrounded by two side
statues and sixteen other images.
The bold colouring of the furniture
is a reminder that this is a
reconstruction done in the Edo
period under the patronage of the
first Tokugawa shogun, Ieyasu.

1895, is enlivened by the twelve subordinate temples in the precincts, many of which are open to the public and which have beautiful gardens. Nanzen-in, the establishment which the former emperor supposedly laboured on, is one of these, and its landscaped garden dates back to the fourteenth century. Another has a garden with a waterfall splashing into it; behind it there is a nineteenth-century red-brick aqueduct whose sole purpose is to transport the water which feeds this 'natural' feature.

Just north of Nanzenji stands the small temple called Eikan-do whose foundation is linked with the same ex-emperor Kameyama who sponsored Nanzenji. The story goes that Kameyama built a detached palace in the vicinity which was bedevilled by misfortunes from the moment it was finished. In 1291 the former monarch called in a priest from Tofukuji temple who successfully rid the place of evil spirits, and as a reward he was given part of the palace for his own residence. It was this that later became Eikan-do. Other versions, however, maintain that the temple's origins are back in the Heian period, and that it was built by a disciple of Kobo Daishi, later becoming a hospital for the poor. Whatever the truth of the matter it is a delightful temple. Its statutary includes a famous image of Amida looking back over his shoulder, as seen by one of the temple's early abbots in a dream. There is also a fine collection of scroll paintings of enormous age depicting herons, peacocks, plum blossoms, a sun rising above a mountain. One long painting depicts nothing but the waves of the sea. All are displayed with insouciant informality, quite unprotected.

Halfway up the mountain behind the temple is a pagoda of the type called *tahoto*, 'pagoda of many treasures', whose design was imported by the two sects, Shingon (to which Eikan-do originally belonged, though it is now of the Jodo sect) and Tendai. This is quite different from the more usual, multi-storey pagoda, and shows close kinship with the pagoda's Indian prototype, the *s'tupa*. In common is the pagoda's cylindrical core under its square roof. In China the core was probably made of stone or brick, under a square and conventionally bracketed roof. In the Japanese version this cylindrical part is made of plaster over wood, and is wrapped around by a square tiled pent roof, possibly because the exposed plaster proved no match for the elements. What remains in the Japanese *tahoto* is a two-storey pagoda with an odd cylindrical bulge between the two roofs.

View of the altar in Eikando temple, near Nanzenji, in north-east Kyoto. Gilded lotus flowers – a popular symbol in Buddhism, with their perfect flowers and their roots in the mud of materiality – are among the many decorative elements.

Daitokuji

The other great Zen foundation in Kyoto is Daitokuji. It was first established in 1319, and though all the original buildings burned down in the fifteenth century, it is an enormous treasure-house of Japanese art, history and spirituality, a testament to the enduring voltage of the Zen sect and to the success with which it sank deep roots in Japanese soil. Like Nanzenji, the heart of the monastery is the strict and decorous progression down a single axis of the primary buildings: two gates, first the Chokushi-mon, then the Sammon, the Buddha Hall and the Lecture Hall. Behind this last are the Hojo, the abbot's quarters. But Daitokuji has flourished to the point where this formal core is almost swallowed up in the abundance of sub-temples all around it, more than twenty of them, each displaying the inspired individuality which was the charming and vital counterweight in Zen to its public and exterior formality.

But even Daitokuji's formal core is infused with vitality. The Triple Gate, for instance: while the lower half dates from 1523–6, the upper storey was added sixty years later by the most celebrated master of the tea ceremony in Japanese history, Sen-no-Rikyu. Among the profusion of paintings and statues is a statue of Rikyu himself, carved by himself. The shogun Hideyoshi was one of Rikyu's tea students, but when, for political reasons, the teacher fell out of favour, Hideyoshi was narrowly prevented from destroying the temple in his fury. This episode is depicted in the recent film *Rikkyu*, directed by Hiroshi Teshigahara, the master of ikebana.

The central image in the Buddha Hall is of Shakyamuni seated in a lotus blossom, and among the memorial tablets in front of it is one for Emperor Go-Daigo, one of the two emperors whom Daitokuji's founder, Daito Kokushi, converted to the Zen sect. Go-Daigo (1288– 1339) is remembered for his success in overwhelming the *bakufu*, the military government, and restoring power, though only briefly, to the throne.

The Lecture Hall or Hatto dates from the seventeenth century, but is probably very similar to the fourteenth-century original, which was the temple's first building. During the Heian period, various architectural devices were employed to extend halls of worship at the front so that they could accommodate larger congregations than could be fitted into a hall of traditional Chinese proportions. The original main hall (no

ABOVE Detail of the elaborations of Zen temple bracketing seen at Daitokuji, the usual features augmented by carved beam-ends and flying rafters with carved noses.

BELOW RIGHT Famous miniature rock garden at Daitokuji's Daisen-in sub-temple which was probably designed by Soami, a celebrated garden designer and painter who died in 1525. Daisen-in also contains some of Soami's paintings.

BELOW LEFT Pond with carp at Rengeji in Kyoto. Carp are bred in Japan in much the same way as pedigree dogs are in Britain, and good specimens change hands for large amounts of money.

longer standing) of Enryaku-ji, the Tendai sect headquarters on Mt Hiei, was an example of such extensions. In the Zen sect, however, only the monks had to be accommodated, and the worship hall resumed its original symmetrical form, with its central, chancel-like space (to express it in the terms of church architecture) and a surrounding ambulatory.

The Hatto at Daitokuji is typical of both Zen Buddha halls and lecture halls in that it is nearly square, five by four bays, covered by a flat ceiling which was painted, like all of them, with a circular painting of a shaggy but not very fearsome-looking dragon. Where the Buddha Hall has an altar platform with images, the Lecture Hall has an elevated pulpit, reached by stairs from both sides and crowned by a throne under a canopy; all these features reinforce the authority of the abbot. The dragon in Daitokuji's Lecture Hall is the work of a famous painter called Kano Tanyu (1602–74). This building is also typical of the new Zen architecture in the exterior bracketing, which takes the complexity at Nara's Toshodaiji, for example, to new extremes of elaboration. The number of bracket complexes sprouting from each capital is doubled, from two to four, and now occupies so much room that the spaces between brackets shrink to insignificance. The timber end slanting down from the interior rafters is doubled, too, and is now carved to end in a point, the line of the beam mimicking that of the roof above.

The effect is more decorative than before; though the way the old aura of muscularity is dissipated in ornamentation for ornamentation's sake has an air of decadence. Indeed in Daitokuji's Hatto, as in other of the late halls, these prettily carved slanting beams are just stuck on the outside, and have no connection with the way the roof is held up. While in this development the Japanese architects were true to their Chinese models, in another way they took artifice further still: when in later centuries they re-roofed these buildings, they replaced the roofs dependent on the visible bracketing with new ones tied together internally, which were structurally independent of the brackets. The outside of a building like Daitokuji's Hatto is in reality a subtle compound of architectural deceit.

The Hojo (abbot's quarters) are decorated with numerous works of art of great antiquity and value, including scenes of China by the dragon painter Kano, and a statue of the temple's founder. It is said of

ABOVE The massed, and badly eroded, images of the Buddhist god of children, Jizo, at Daitokuji. When images (or lanterns, or *torii* gates) are found in such numbers it is always a sign that they have been given by the faithful. These have been decorated by the faithful, as well, mostly by women who have lost their children through death or abortion.

BELOW RIGHT Part of the stone (*karesansui*) garden of Daitokuji's Zuiho-in sub-temple: precisely modulated patterns of gravel swirl liquidly around a mossy rock. Opinions differ as to whether gardens of this sort tell a specific story in which each element plays a clearly prescribed role, or whether their significance is far more elusive.

BELOW LEFT Another view of the *karesansui* garden at Daitoku-ji's Zuiho-in, with well-disciplined topiary behind.

the founder that he spent twenty years before founding the temple living with beggars under Kyoto's Gojo Bridge to deepen his spiritual understanding. The two gardens alongside the Hojo are of great fame, both being of the *karesansui* or 'dry' style, comprising white gravel and stones, with shrubs in the background. The east one, said to be the work of one of the most famous of all garden designers, Kobori Enshu (1576–1647), uses the technique of 'borrowed scenery': the eye is led from the gravel in the foreground via the shrubs behind, to the mountains in the distance, which lend their vast scale to the tiny creation. The original effect is hard to imagine today as the view is badly blotted by telephone wires and other modern accretions.

These are the central buildings and spaces of Daitokuji, but the sub-temples are also full of delights – buildings, gardens, works of art. Among the most noted are Shinju-an, behind the abbot's quarters, which contains a statue of Ikkyu (1394–1481), the most celebrated Zen master of Daitokuji, and a garden which is said by some to be the best in Japan. Juko-in, west of the abbot's quarters, holds the tomb of Sen-no-Rikyu, attesting further to the deep interpenetration of Rikyu's tea ceremony and the Rinzai school of Zen which Daitokuji represents. The Koho-an in the west of the monastery is practically a monument to the garden designer Kobori Enshu: seven ceremonial tea rooms here are of his design, while the garden is also his, and he and his family are interred in the south-west corner.

The garden on the east side of Daisen-in, the sub-temple to the west of Shinju-an, is another of Japan's most famous and is focused around a single rock. The flow of gravel across the tiny space has been interpreted as representing the flow of life from the happy torrents of impulsive youth, through the cares and sufferings of age, to the emptiness of the garden's southern end, where there are no more rocks and no more nothing. In the words of Ikkyu: 'All things inevitably turn to nothingness, and this "turning to nothingness" means a return to original being.'

The most famous rock garden in Kyoto is the one at Ryoanji temple. Like many other noted monuments around the world, the fame of Ryoanji has been somewhat counterproductive, both because it is inundated by visitors who seriously imperil whatever serenity the place once had, and because many of those who come, the foreigners especially, have such inflated expectations that they cannot fail to be

Most visitors are too preoccupied by the stone garden to discover that Ryoanji, a small, modest temple, is surrounded by a splendid and much more conventional garden, of which this is part.

disappointed. It is a modest Zen temple of the fifteenth century, with a small garden of raked gravel containing fifteen rocks. Numerous attempts have been made to explain what this garden is all about, but as in the case of the best classical music or abstract painting, this is ultimately futile. One Zen master commented that it takes thirty-five years to learn how to sit in Zen meditation, and a similar period would probably be useful to get an insight into Ryoanji's garden.

The importation of Zen was one great result of the chaotic conditions that followed the end of the Heian period. Another was the creation of native Japanese schools of Buddhism which spoke to the spiritual needs not of the ruling class but of the ordinary people. The Nichiren sect was one of these, but it has no significant headquarters in Kyoto. Another whose presence bulks hugely in the modern city is the Jodo Shin sect. This was the creation of the disciples of a priest called Shinran (1173–1262) whose life straddled the divide between the end of the Heian and the beginning of the Kamakura periods. Shinran was himself indebted to the teaching of a priest forty years his senior called Honen. Both, in the tradition of Buddhist pioneers from Shakyamuni himself onwards, explored all currently available manifestations of wisdom and found them wanting. Honen's insight, after years of seeking, was that true salvation was to be found very simply by the endless repetition of the words *Namu Amida Butsu*, meaning 'Glory to Amida Buddha'. Shinran basically took the same position, though, as later expounded by his followers, what was required was faith in the saving power of Amida, whereupon repetition of the formula became the natural expression of a grateful heart. As is clear, the practice of the two was the same; and in contrast to the philosophical intricacies and monastic demands of Zen, this was a form of Buddhism which was wonderfully simple, one which the most unlettered countryman could master and practice. In the apocalyptic days of the thirteenth century, when the established order was crumbling and everything indicated that the world was coming to an end, the audience for this wonderful message was huge.

And huge were the temples they built to house them. Honen's followers formed the Jodo-shu, the Pure Land sect, whose headquarters is Chion-in, in Kyoto. Shinran's founded the Jodo Shin-shu, the True Pure Land sect, and called its head temple Honganji, which was located at Yamashina, east of the city, at the site of Shinran's grave. Later they removed to the centre of the city where a schism rendered the sect into

ABOVE LEFT The most famous *karesansui* garden of them all: the one at Ryoanji temple, which comprises fifteen rocks, arranged in groups of seven, five and three. From whatever point one looks at the garden, there is always one rock hidden, though whether this means anything is debatable.

ABOVE RIGHT Bamboo pipes bring fresh spring water to a basin in the garden at Ryoanji; the dipper is used for ritual purification.

BELOW The interior of Ryoanji, a small temple in the north of Kyoto famous for its stone garden. The partitioning of the broad interior space by sliding doors, *fusuma*, is typical of classical domestic interiors, as is the *tokonoma* alcove at the far end, where flowers and a scroll painting are usually displayed.

two parts, both of which occupy massive and remarkably similar temples not far north of Kyoto railway station.

Similar to each other, Nishi- and Higashi-Honganji are quite different from any other Buddhist temples established up to that date. The traditional south-oriented axis is quite done away with. The temples consist of two vast halls, both facing east, linked by a roofed corridor. The larger is on the right as one faces them from the east and is called the Taishido, Founder's Hall, because it is dedicated to Shinran. The smaller is the Amida-do, dedicated to Amida, but though smaller its dignity is rescued by its being two storeys higher than the Taishido, and more heavily ornamented. The two halls were not always this big: the ones of Higashi-Honganji were originally just three bays square, but as the numbers of believers increased they were gradually enlarged to accommodate them.

There is something repellent about the gargantuan scale of these establishments, but they nevertheless have an interest of their own. With their great congregations they are more analogous to a theatre, a palace or indeed a Christian cathedral than to other temples. The huge *raido* running across the west end of the hall functions like a stage, and at the start of a service the depth of it is closed off from view. At a certain point the doors are pulled back to reveal the brilliantly illuminated altar, image and lamps. It is quite a spectacle.

Nishi-Honganji, also called the 'original', has various other interesting structures within its walls. One is the fabulous Higurashi-mon, 'End-of-day Gate', so called because it is so richly adorned with decoration that one could look at it all day without seeing all there is to see – like the architecture at Nikko, to which it is closely related. But the most interesting building at Nishi-Honganji unfortunately seems wholly impenetrable. This is the Hiunkaku, 'Floating Cloud Pavilion', formerly a country villa of the shogun Hideyoshi, and believed to have been removed to this site in 1630. It is one of the masterpieces of informality which the Japanese achieved in this period in residential buildings. The style of almost haphazard eclecticism is called *sukiya* and was strongly influenced by the aesthetic of the tea cottage. Besides its beautiful paintings and tea chamber, the house incorporates the exotic Boat Docking room, into which it was possible to row from the small pond outside. Today it is perhaps only crowned heads of state on formal visits who are granted a sight of Hiunkaku.

RIGHT The monumental halls and empty graveled spaces of Nishi-Honganji make a curious contrast to the hedonistic liveliness of its entrance gate. The hall on the right, the larger of the two, is the *Taishido* or Founder's Hall, where huge congregations gather; on the left is the *Amida-do* or Amida Hall.

OVERLEAF ABOVE Gilt, black lacquer and intensely detailed representational carving characterize the *Kara Mon*, 'Chinese Gate', of central Kyoto's Nishi-Honganji, a typical construction of the early Edo period.

OVERLEAF BELOW LEFT Detail of the joinery of Nishi-Honganji. The tradition of Japanese carpentry has always found its highest fulfilment in temple design and building, and precise and intricate jointing techniques are at the heart of the tradition.

OVERLEAF BELOW RIGHT The stone garden was perhaps the most characteristic creation of Kyoto in the classical period and there are dozens of specimens to admire. This one is at Nishi-Honganji, with the temple's buildings seen in the background.

ABOVE Another view of the *Kara Mon* of Nishi-Honganji, with its curved hood emphasized by a tiled and decorated roof ridge.

RIGHT Trough and dippers for ritual purification at Nishi-Honganji, under their own roof. The size of the trough and the number of dippers is one indication of the temple's popularity.

ABOVE The *Tsukimidai* or moon-viewing platform of Ginkakuji, the Temple of the Silver Pavilion, is no more than an immaculately shaped cone of gravel flattened at the top. One of the hardest of Kyoto's stone gardens to comprehend, it strikingly sets off the beautiful climbing garden of trees and shrubs beyond.

BELOW Silver in name only, the pavilion at the heart of Ginkakuji, built in the late fifteenth century, epitomizes medieval Japanese architectural taste at its most refined: modest almost to the point of shabbiness, astringent, supremely delicate in proportion and detailing. The ground floor is closed by the paper-covered shutters, *shoji*, an early use of what later became a ubiquitous feature of Japanese houses. Like the earlier Golden Pavilion, the upper windows are cusped, Zen style, but these, too, are shuttered with paper screens.

The Golden and Silver Pavilions

By the middle of the fourteenth century the wheel of fortune came round again and political power returned to the old capital, and to a newly ascendant family of nobles, the Ashikaga. For the 200 chaotic years of the Muromachi period the Ashikaga shoguns did their best to hold sway, and no sooner did they feel themselves secure than they, too, began to build themselves simulacra of heaven. These were the Golden Pavilion and the Silver Pavilion. Both are famous, evanescently beautiful, and as vain as peacocks. Built on opposite sides of the city, both were in fact and intention exquisite country retreats, and were only converted into temples on the deaths of the powerful men who built them.

Kinkakuji, the Temple of the Golden Pavilion, has had the stormier history of the two and is the more immediately awe-inspiring. The original villa on this site was built in the thirteenth century, but it was the third Ashikaga shogun Yoshimitsu (1358–1408) who built the pavilion itself and laid out the garden, in 1394, and whiled away his retirement there. Even aside from the fact of its being covered in gold leaf, the pavilion is an extraordinary building, because each of its three storeys is designed in a different style. The ground floor, with a railing that overlooks the Kyoho-chi pond, is in the palace style called Shinden-zukuri; the first floor is in the style of a samurai residence; while the second floor borrows the motifs of a Zen temple, particularly the rich panelling of the doors and the cusped arches of the windows. The roof is covered with shingles and topped with a phoenix. The difference in taste between Byodo-in and Kinkakuji is mostly explained by the influence of Zen, whose priests were advisors to the shoguns on all aesthetic matters. The greater confidence of the later buildings is seen in their deft balancing of the different qualities of Chinese and Japanese taste, so that while the massing of the temple has a Chinese solidity, the delicacy of its members and detailing betrays an unmistakably Japanese sensibility.

The present building dates from 1955. The original pavilion was deliberately burned down by a priest in 1950, an event fictionalized by Yukio Mishima in his novel *Kinkakuji*. He interpreted it as an act of fury directed against the materialism of modern Japan. It was rebuilt with painstaking fidelity and regilded in 1987, with gold leaf five times thicker than before. The other notable structure on the site is the

charming thatched tea cottage called Sekka-tei. The grounds are a delight, though not as great as the landscaped beauty of Ginkakuji.

Ginkakuji, the Temple of the Silver Pavilion, is located at the north end of the 'Philosophy Path' that leads up from Nanzenji and Eikando. It was built in 1480, in frank emulation of the achievement of the Golden Pavilion, but despite the name this structure was never covered with silver. The pavilion itself is almost comically modest, though possessed of the same fragile elegance as its older relation. And the garden is stupendous, especially in autumn. Between the pavilion and the Buddha Hall is one of Kyoto's oddest expanses of artistic stones, including a flat-topped cone of gravel known as Kogetsu-dai, 'Moon-viewing platform'.

The Silver Pavilion was built by and for the benefit of Yoshimasa, the eighth Ashikaga shogun and the most luxurious of them all. 'I love my hut at the foot of the Moon-Awaiting Mountain and the reflection of the sinking sky,' he wrote, as his nation went up in flames that were not to be put out for over a hundred years.

Kinkakuji's Golden Pavilion in the snow. Photo © Takeji Iwamiya.

4 Kamakura and Beyond

Buddha image at Kenchoji, Kamakura, showing the decorated, coffered ceiling peculiar to the architecture of this sect. On the right of the image, resting on an ornate red cushion on a stand, is the cylindrical gong the priest strikes to accompany or punctuate his chanting of the sutras.

Compared to Kyoto, it is very easy to get to grips with the history of Kamakura. The place flourished once and once only. It started life as a fishing village, was unexpectedly turned into the nation's *de facto* capital, and then, after a century and a half, returned to its original state. It did enjoy a brief revival a century or so after that, when it was made the headquarters of the government of eastern Japan, but this was no more than a coda to the glory that came before.

Today Kamakura is a major tourist attraction as well as a dormitory suburb – 'bed town' in the pithier Japanese-English phrase – for Tokyo and Yokohama. But it has never regained centrality, and is never likely to. There is much less to see here than in Kyoto, but all that there is belongs to that moment of glory, so it is possible here to gain a fairly powerful impression of the city as it was then.

Kamakura is a delightful place to visit. It is only an hour by train from central Tokyo, but the physical features that persuaded the Minamoto chieftain Yoritomo to base himself here at the end of the twelfth century – the small but steep and impenetrably wooded mountains and the sea – have also kept the modern megalopolis at arm's length. Despite the continuing incursions of property developers, whose estates of commuter housing spoil some of its hidden valleys, it preserves an atmosphere of its own. The old monuments, the temples and shrines, have not been drowned out entirely by modern buildings; the hills are full of hidden pathways which lead to half-forgotten relics of the Middle Ages; and the medieval plan of the town, a miniature copy of Kyoto's, still governs the way it is laid out today.

Kamakura is dominated by a broad main street which leads from the sea dead straight for most of the way to the *torii* entrance to the principal shrine. The road is called Wakamiya-oji. The shrine in which it culminates is called Tsurugaoka Hachiman-gu, the shrine of Hachiman, God of War in the Shinto pantheon, on the Hill of Cranes. The first version of this shrine was built somewhere else altogether by an earlier Minamoto, but Yoritomo removed it to this site after his clan crushed the Taira and he, as shogun, moved his headquarters to Kamakura in 1191. It was the least he could do for the god who had looked after him so well.

Like all the best major shrines, Hachiman-gu is an immensely lively centre of popular devotion, full of interest and charm. Its grounds are enormous and incorporate a small museum of antiquities, a martial arts gymnasium, a garden full of winter peonies, and a museum of modern art which was one of the key works of early post-war modern Japanese architecture, in addition to a profusion of shrine buildings. The heart of the shrine is reached by steep steps into the Hill of Cranes, past the roofed open-air stage where Shinto dancing is performed on feast days. Activities to which the shrine is host at different times of the year include outdoor tea ceremonies, a midsummer exhibition of paintings done on lanterns which are erected along the pathways, tournaments of *yabusame*, the ancient art of archery on horseback, and the festivities of New Year when the grounds fill up with stalls selling food and drink, and hundreds of thousands of people pour in to pay their respects to the god and pray for a fortunate year.

And besides all these there are the weddings, the baby blessings, the presentation of children aged 7, 5 and 3 which take place in the autumn, all arrayed in their best kimono like miniature samurai and courtesans. At the foot of the steps up to the shrine proper, on the left, is a vast and ancient ginkgo tree, planted here to mark the place where the third Kamakura shogun was murdered by his nephew – the first augury of serious dynastic troubles to come. The shrine buildings are painted in that distinctive shade of vermilion lacquer peculiar to shrines. They are roofed and detailed just like Buddhist temple buildings, but inside there is the characteristic Shinto din of drums being banged and ancient creaky instruments being played, the spectacle of the pious having paper wands waved over them by dignified young priests in white kimono and ice-green *hakama* (divided skirts). To the side of the main buildings is a small, empty plot of land, cordoned by sacred rope, the site reserved for the ritual rebuilding that never happens in shrines these days except at Ise (the present main buildings date from 1828). Also nearby, at the top of a little shaded hillock, is a small *kitsune* or fox sub-shrine; as in all such shrines, the approach path is lined with miniature *torii* gates. At the base of the Hill of Cranes and over to the right, as one faces it with the town behind, is an exquisite sub-shrine called Wakamiya (junior shrine) painted in black lacquer, which was built in 1624.

It was not whimsy that caused Yoritomo to extend the approach road to Hachiman-gu all the way down some three kilometres to the sea shore. Nowadays Kamakura's curving sandy beach is no more than a popular though polluted summertime magnet for sunbathers and

LEFT Cusped window typical of the Zen style at Kenchoji. The carved stone plinths on which the posts rest are also clearly seen. The window is closed from inside by sliding wooden shutters.

RIGHT The *torii* or entrance gate at Hachiman-gu, painted bright vermilion like most *torii* around the country. The top horizontal member curves upwards at the ends, unlike the level beam at Ise, demonstrating the influence of Chinese style on shrine design.

BELOW One of the main buildings at Kenchoji, the principal Zen temple of Kamakura, which illustrates some characteristics of the Zen architectural style: the pent roof, the use of brackets between as well as on top of the columns, the setting of the building on a stone podium with the posts resting on carved stone plinths. The curved hood or cusped gable on the main roof is an incongruous Edo period addition.

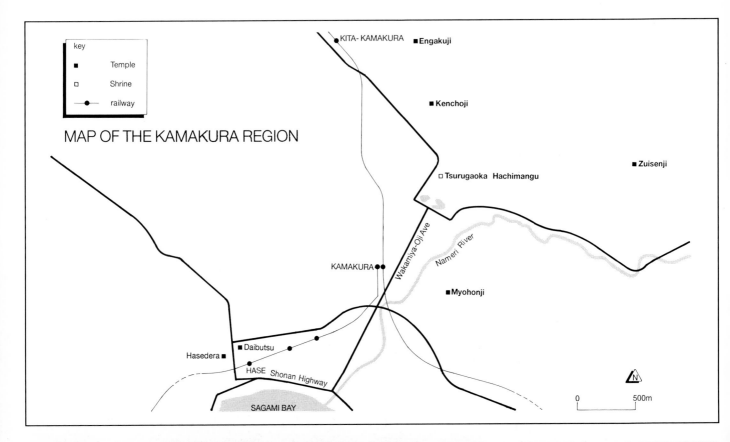

MAP OF THE KAMAKURA REGION

key
■ Temple
□ Shrine
●— railway

KITA- KAMAKURA
■ Engakuji
■ Kenchoji
■ Zuisenji
□ Tsurugaoka Hachimangu
Wakamiya-Oji Ave
Nameri River
KAMAKURA
■ Myohonji
Hasedera ■
■ Daibutsu
HASE   Shonan Highway
SAGAMI BAY
0   500m
N

windsurfers, but in the thirteenth century, when an artificial harbour was built here, it was for a time the busiest port in the land. And here it was that the Chinese priest Tao-Lung, Daigaku-zenji in Japanese, arrived bearing news of the Ch'an (Zen) school of Buddhism.

Indirectly the Mongol hordes were to be thanked for this event, for the missionaries were fleeing the destruction caused by the invading armies from the north. Kamakura was the beneficiary, becoming the first Japanese home of Zen, and it is still home to some of the most important and flourishing Zen temples. Three of them at least are worthy of mention. Kenchoji is not the oldest, but it is foremost in the Kamakura hierarchy and it is also the grandest, the one most redolent of Kamakura as capital. It was founded in 1253 by Tao-Lung after he succeeded in converting the ruling member of the Hojo family (which had already supplanted the Minamoto as the country's military governors). Set among high paulownia trees a kilometre south of Kita [= North]-Kamakura station, it still has a community of monks who stay several years undergoing the harsh training in *zazen* (meditation) and *koan* practice before departing to take over smaller Zen temples around the country. Like Nanzenji and Daitokuji in Kyoto its buildings are lined up in a single axis, most of them dating from its faithful reconstruction in the seventeenth century. Unlike the great Kyoto establishments, however, it lacks the proliferation of sub-temples which testify to Kyoto's enduring importance down the centuries as a cultural centre.

Engakuji or Enkakuji was founded thirty years after Kenchoji and spreads across the hill to the east of Kita-Kamakura station; in fact its grounds are bisected by the railway line. The steep contours give this temple an intimacy Kenchoji lacks, though several of its best buildings were destroyed in the earthquake of 1923. The most famous structure is the Shariden or Relic Hall, a national treasure, which is said to contain one of Shakyamuni's teeth. The hard times on which Kamakura's temples fell may be responsible for the uncouth thatched roof over this building, which was probably covered by a more elegant, gently sloping tile roof when it was first built. Engakuji's bronze bell, housed in a bell tower to the right as one enters, is also a national treasure, and is the largest in Kamakura.

The third temple does not rank among the great houses like the two above, but demonstrates the sensitive use made by the Zen architects of

ABOVE The Kara-mon, Chinese-style, gate at Nikko's Toshogu Shrine, with another shrine building beyond. Like Nikko's other famous gate, Yomeimon, Kara-mon is unique both in general design and intensity of decoration. The cusped gables are more steeply arched than in other gates of this style. The carvings that crowd the eaves include auspicious birds, dragons, lions and characters from Chinese legends. There are no motifs from Japanese mythology, emphasizing the self-conscious foreignness of the design.

ABOVE RIGHT The most famous carvings at Nikko are these charming and humorous representations of the Three Wise Monkeys.

BELOW RIGHT Carved Chinese lion among the fantastic bestiary of Nikko.

a good location. This is Zuisenji, tucked away among secluded valleys in the east of the city, which was founded in 1327 by a priest called Soshi, of whom a noted wooden image survives in the Founder's Hall. The temple's diminutive buildings have recently been rebuilt in perfect taste, but just as famous as these, and as popular, are the beautifully laid-out gardens, full of plum blossom in February and flaming red *momoji* (Japanese maple) leaves in the autumn.

Kamakura's most illustrious relic of its glorious past is the Daibutsu, the Great Buddha, over to the west: the second tallest historic Buddha in the country after Todaiji's, and a much better work of art than that one. A bronze figure over eleven metres high, it was said to have been cast in the mid-thirteenth century and was originally enclosed in its own Buddha Hall, as Todaiji's is. This was carried away by a tidal wave in 1495, however, and the Buddha has sat in the open ever since. Now it is hard to imagine him any other way than resplendent against the green hills and blue sky.

Nearby is the Hasedera temple of the Jodo sect which dates from about the same era, whose Kannon image is a massive 9.3 metres tall and was carved from a single camphor tree. Hasedera is also famous for its hundreds of images of the Buddhist deity Jizo, brought by mothers whose children have died in infancy or women who have had abortions, as prayers for their babies' souls. Many are decorated in the most pathetic way with little bibs and woolly hats and set about with toys.

Kamakura also has numerous temples of the Nichiren sect, the indigenous sect that sprang out of the chaos at the start of the Kamakura period and which had a strongly populist and nationalistic slant. While the Zen sect characteristically built its monasteries in the tranquillity of the hills, Nichiren, the founder, built in the middle of the city, where the tradesmen and the urban poor who were his natural congregation could most easily assemble. The temples themselves are not noted for the seductiveness of their architecture, although Nichiren's is the only Japanese sect which continued to favour the pagoda. An exception to the rule of earnest drabness is Myohonji, near the centre of Kamakura, founded by one of Nichiren's disciples, and which, although a stone's throw from the middle of town, has the benefit of a site made noble by tall paulownia trees.

Nichiren's importance as a religious figurehead has endured. The most successful lay-Buddhist sect in modern Japan, Soka Gakkai, with

ABOVE Carved animal reliefs under the eaves at Nikko.

BELOW LEFT The overall impression of Toshogu is overwhelming; the charm of the shrine is best found in its details, like this relief of flowers and leaves.

BELOW RIGHT More decorative detailing at Nikko.

ABOVE The Yomei-mon, together with Kara-mon the most heavily decorated feature of the Toshogu Shrine. In Yomei-mon hardly a single beam, bracket or panel is left uncarved. Like Kara-mon this is in 'Chinese-style', but it is a fanciful imagining of Chinese style rather than an imitation of the real thing.

BELOW The mixture of Shinto and Buddhist elements at Nikko is thorough and deliberate. The bronze *torii* here is typical of Shinto: behind it is a Zen-style sutra depository with pent roof and windows with cusped arches. Such a repository is ordinarily found only in a temple.

millions of adherents, its own significant political party and immense wealth, is a modern offshoot of the Nichiren sect.

Architecture after Kamakura

'By the standards of Western criticism,' wrote Alexander Soper, the most authoritative foreign historian of Japanese architecture, 'Japanese Buddhist architecture completed the last major phase of its evolution in the fourteenth century.' It is a judgement which is at first sight surprising. Buddhism did not cease to flourish after this date, nor did new temples cease to be built or old ones reconstructed. Soper's irrefutable point is that as a living, imaginative force, Buddhist architecture after Kamakura began to wither. The prototypes by then were all in place. New transfusions of inspiration from the continent were no longer available after the shambles of the Mongol conquest, and when, in Ming, they became available, they were no longer wanted because Japan had shut itself away. As in other spheres of Japanese art, the Noh drama or the Kabuki, the repertoire was set. What remained to those who came after was to mix, to refine, to ornament, sometimes to spoil.

To endorse Soper's point is to run the risk of seeming to say that beyond those cultural cauldrons, Nara, Kyoto and Kamakura, and outside those given dates, there is nothing worthy of notice. This is obviously not true: all over the islands of Japan except for Hokkaido (which was not developed until the latter part of the nineteenth century) there are numerous temples full of charm and interest: from the dilapidated relics on Sado Island, to the mighty Soto Zen temple headquarters at Eiheiji in Fukui Prefecture, to the temples in the far north along the route taken by the Haiku poet Basho. Each is a variation on one or other of the developments which have been discussed.

One huge establishment stands outside that framework, however, and it constitutes both a final efflorescence and a declaration of bankcruptcy. This is the Toshogu shrine at Nikko. Nothing could be more splendid – 'Don't say *kekko* (wonderful) until you've seen Nikko', runs the Japanese saying. At the same time, as the mausoleum of a dead dictator, nothing could be a greater trivialization of the Buddhist theme. After this, Buddhist architecture in Japan had nowhere to go but down.

LEFT Five-storey pagoda at Oku-no-in, in Nikko, in the mountains north of the main shrine compound. Like the other shrine buildings it is heavily decorated. In contrast to earlier pagodas such as that of Horyuji (Chapter 1), all the roofs are of the same size.

ABOVE AND BELOW RIGHT Details of decorative work at Nikko.

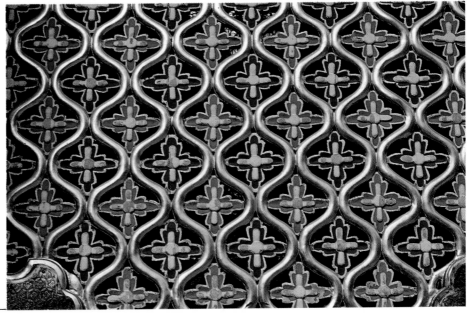

Ieyasu was the third of the three great shoguns whose collective achievement was to bring peace and order to Japan. So well did he do his work, so painstakingly did he bind the rival fiefdoms together with the ties of taxation and obligation, that Japan's peace and isolation endured under the (increasingly nominal) rule of his heirs, for two and a half centuries. Here, then, was a man worthy of a decent burial, and after his death in 1613 his grandson Iemitsu set out to provide it. The site chosen was in the mountains to the north of Tokyo, an area of crisp air, delicious water and rich alpine scenery.

The work commenced in 1634. Incredibly, considering the achievement, it was finished just two years later, in time for the twentieth anniversary of Ieyasu's death. Years earlier the emperor had post-humously conferred on Ieyasu the resounding title Tosho Daigongen, Buddha Incarnate, Sun God of the East, a form which yoked the highest terms of esteem from both Japan's religions. Iemitsu set about building a mausoleum which would do justice to it. Accordingly, Toshogu shrine is neither temple nor shrine but a hubristic apotheosis of both. Every device in the repertory of Buddhist and Shinto architecture is drafted into service. The entrance is marked by a stone *torii* gate, but shortly beyond that and to the left is a five-storey pagoda. The site climbs into the hills in a manner typical of Shinto, as Hachiman-gu in Kamakura does. There is accommodation for votive animals – stables for the sacred horses – which is also common in Shinto. But the shrine's plan exploits the architectonic rhythms typical of a temple, with a succession of roofed gates culminating in the Hall of Worship. There is a place for visitors to purify their hands and mouths in running water in the ritual manner before entering the holy precincts, as in a shrine; but there is also a *sutra* repository and a bell house. The Oku-no-In – the Deep Shrine up in the mountains – exploits the Shinto sense that sanctity resides in the deep heart of the mountain, but in its midst is another (Buddhist) pagoda.

The most famous thing about Nikko is its ornamentation. It is possibly the busiest piece of architecture in the world. And who can deny that it is truly fantastic? The Higurashi-mon, 'End of Day Gate', of Nishi-Honganji in Kyoto is so called because one could stare at it all day without seeing all there is to see, without growing tired of it. At Nikko one could stare all year. Restraint, understatement, nuance, astringent melancholy – these favourite Japanese qualities, found alike

in such masterpieces as Ise and Ryoanji – have no place at all in Nikko. The colours scream. The extravagance is hard to comprehend. Gold is here in abundance, 2,489,000 sheets of it, each twenty-five square centimetres, enough to cover twenty-four hectares. The violent blues and reds and greens clash frenzedly. Underneath, everywhere, is the deep, slightly sinister gleam of black lacquer, alongside expanses of blinding white. Every piece of every surface is carved, painted, gilded until nothing more is possible. It seems extraordinary that the buildings can stand up under the weight of it.

What can be seen to suffer are the architectural forms which have to carry it all. They cannot sustain such a surfeit. Take the Yomei-mon, for example. In a sense this is the climax of one's experience of the shrine. Nikko, the place, is written in the characters for sunlight. Ieyasu was deified as the 'Sun God of the East'. All traditional nationalistic connections between the sun, Japan as its origin, Ameterasu the Sun Goddess as the country's founder, were invoked in the cause of his greater glory. And here it is, the Gate of Sunlight, the entrance to the Holy of Holies. In essence it is the traditional entrance gate of a temple with the *irimoya* hipped-cum-gable roof. Enriching that, in a way that was to become enormously popular in the Edo period (and was inserted, for example, in the Edo period rebuilding of Todaiji's Buddha Hall), was an extra curving gable at the front called a *karamon*. The gate itself is three bays wide, and the roof is supported on the customary bracketing. But the bracketing has gone mad: wildly decorated, it goes on and on, interrupted by a narrow upper-storey balcony surmounted by curved beams. It grows out of all control, and what is forfeited is the over-all balance of the whole structure. It looks like an erupting souffle.

Nikko represents the grand finale of the long and rich tradition of Buddhist architecture in Japan: a formidable peak of technical achievement to rank with the gilded extravagances of any other civilization, but also a cul-de-sac beyond which further creative development of the temple was to prove impossible. From this pinnacle, or this dead end, whichever we find ourselves regarding it, we look back over the course that tradition has taken since the building of Horyuji with enormous admiration for the passion, the imagination and the accomplishment of the island carpenters.

PREVIOUS PAGE The rear of the sanctuary at Toshogu Shrine in Ueno, central Tokyo, which in style is first cousin to the Toshogu Shrine at Nikko, though on a far more modest scale. It is the most historically important building in Ueno Park, north of central Tokyo.

Travellers' Information

Planning the Trip

Getting There
Narita, Tokyo's international airport, is the principal point of entry to Japan. Osaka Airport, served by international carriers from Los Angeles as well as Asian centres such as Hong Kong and Bangkok, is more convenient for Kyoto and Nara, but at present is not a practical option for most visitors. Narita is 60km north of Tokyo and the trip into the centre of Tokyo by train or limousine bus takes up to two hours. In a year or two a new international airport will open outside Osaka which will make access to Kyoto and Nara from abroad more straightforward.

When to Go
The weather is pleasantest and most reliable between October and December, with many warm, dry, fine days. Everybody else knows this, too, however, so places like Kyoto throng with visitors, Japanese and foreign. Spring, from March to the end of May, is also pleasantly mild, though often wet. June, July and August are hot and humid, August being the worst. A short rainy season, *tsuyu* in Japanese, occurs in June and July and is worth avoiding. Winter is often extremely dry and fine on the east coast, snowy on the west, cold everywhere, though no worse than New York.

Travel Documents
Holders of British, Irish, French, Swiss, West German and Austrian passports can stay up to 180 days without a visa. Most other West Europeans and South Americans can stay for up to 60 days, and New Zealanders for up to 30. Australians and North Americans need a 60-day visa from a Japanese embassy or consulate; these can be extended a maximum of two times, to a total of 180 days. Vaccination certificates are only required for those entering from areas where cholera and/or typhoid are endemic.

Costs
The frugal and penny-pinching can have a holiday in Japan without breaking the bank, but whether they will enjoy themselves is another question. Nearly all the agreeable things in Japan cost a lot: attractive *ryokan* (inns), good restaurants, comfortable travel, craft items, antiques. Some of the more interesting temples charge 1,000 yen or even more for admission. The two best ways to economize are by buying a rail pass before setting out and seeking out reasonably-priced accommodation. In restaurants, lunch is a much better deal than dinner.

Travel within Japan

Domestic flights leave from Haneda Airport, near central Tokyo on the bay. Buses go there directly from Narita. The *Shinkansen*, often called the bullet train in English, covers the distance from Tokyo to Kyoto in under four hours but is expensive. Travellers on a budget prefer the night buses operated by Japan Railways which travel to Kyoto and elsewhere for a fraction of the *Shinkansen* fare. They leave from the Yaesu side of Tokyo Station at around 11pm. An economical way to see the country is to buy a rail pass, available for 7, 14 or 21 days. These can only be bought outside Japan, and are not valid for travel on the numerous private lines. More details are available from the Japan Travel Bureau.

Many places of interest within the Kyoto-Nara region can be reached by train, the private lines being cheaper and often more useful than JR, the recently-privatised national line. Kyoto's modest subway is a good way of avoiding streets which are always congested. Buses are available to the more out-of-the-way sites; ask at Kyoto's Tourist Information Centre near the main railway station for details. Taxis are expensive but useful in a pinch.

Kamakura is one hour from Tokyo Station by train. Taxi is the only practical way round the town's attractions for those in a hurry, as they are well spread out. Nikko is 1 hour 45 minutes from Tokyo's Asakusa Station on the private Tobu Line. The town and mausoleum can be explored on foot.

Accommodation

The range is vast, both in style and price. A small *tatami* – floored room in a simple inn can cost as little as 4,000 yen; a room in a first-class hotel can cost five times as much or even more, while a first-class *ryokan* may be ten times as much.

For practicality and economy the business hotels found all over Japan are recommended. Room rates start at about 5,000 yen and though the rooms are often tiny they offer the conveniences of an ordinary western hotel, though they score nil for atmosphere. For the same sort of price you can stay in a cheap *ryokan* or a *minshuku* – literally 'people's inn' – in which the rooms are Japanese style, with very little furniture. The beds are futons stored during the day in the built-in closets, and the breakfast, routinely included in the price, is Japanese style, too. Difficult for those with an aversion to living on the floor or eating with chopsticks, inns of this sort offer a fascinating slice of ordinary Japanese life. Try asking about economical *ryokan* and *minshuku* at the Tourist Information Centre. Kyoto in particular has numerous fairly basic *ryokan* which are nonetheless picturesque and welcoming to foreigners.

Those with larger budgets have the possibility of staying in more elegant *ryokan* – about 12,000 to 50,000 yen and more per night – which offer an unforgettable taste of the traditional Japanese lifestyle at its most refined. Kyoto has the best and most famous. Here, too, however, you will spend most of the time on the mats. For the same sort of high prices, first class Japanese hotels are largely indistinguishable from those in the West. Whatever your budget or preference, you will be unlikely to find yourself in accommodation that is not spotlessly clean.

General Information

Money
The yen is denominated in 1, 5, 10, 50, 100 and 500 yen coins, and 1,000, 5,000 and 10,000 yen notes. At the time of going to press US $1 fetched about 170 yen. Changing travellers' cheques in currencies other than yen takes a lot of time outside the centre of Tokyo, and changing cash in currencies other than the US dollar, sterling or deutschmark can be an even bigger problem. Japan is probably the safest place in the world to carry cash around. American Express, Carte Blanche, Diners Club, MasterCard/Access and Visa Cards can be used in the major hotels and expensive shops but are greeted by blank stares elsewhere. Tipping is practically unheard of, and never expected.

Timezone
Japan is eight hours ahead of the UK in British summertime, nine hours ahead in winter.

Access to Temples and Shrines
Most famous temples charge for admission though the rates vary widely, from a nominal 100 yen to 1,000 yen and more. Entrance to shrines is normally free, though there are exceptions such as Kasuga Shrine in Nara. Shoes must be removed before entering temple buildings, and photographing interiors is often frowned on.

Souvenirs
Kyoto and Kamakura are full of tempting craft items such as pottery, lacquerware, kimono and *obi* (kimono sashes), swords, wind-chimes, kites and innumerable delicately made knick-knacks. There are few real bargains; Tokyo's flea markets, held on Sundays, offer the best possibilities.

Tourist Information
The best sources of detailed information for foreign visitors are the Tourist Information Centres (TICs), one each in Tokyo, Kyoto and Narita Airport. They provide free maps, train schedules, accommodation lists and practical mini-guides to particular destinations. Japan Travel Phone is an information service in English: in Tokyo call 502-1461, in Kyoto 371-5649.

Further Reading

The Art and Architecture of Japan, Robert Treat Paine and Alexander Soper, Pelican, Third Edition 1981. Two books in one, both authoritative and detailed on the development of Japan's art and architecture.

What is Japanese Architecture?, Kazuo Nishi and Kazuo Hozumi, tr. H. Mack Norton, Kodansha International, Tokyo, 1985. Heavily illustrated, readable survey of traditional Japanese architecture in all aspects.

The Genius of Japanese Carpentry: An Account of a Temple's Construction, S. Azby Brown, Kodansha International, 1989. Detailed account of the living tradition of temple carpentry and the reconstruction of one of the buildings of Nara's Yakushiji Temple.

Cultural Atlas of Japan, Martin Collcutt, Marius Jansen and Isao Kumakura, Phaidon Press, 1988. Lavishly illustrated, many extraordinary maps.

The Heibonsha Survey of Japanese Art, various authors, Weatherhill/Heibonsha. Thirty separate titles on Japanese traditional arts by Japanese authorities. Individual titles include Edo Architecture: Katsura and Nikko; and The Garden Art of Japan.

Historical Kyoto, Herbert E. Plutschow, The Japan Times Ltd., 1983. Not a practical guide, but lots of background on the history and myths of Kyoto.

Historical Nara, Companion volume to the above.

Kyoto: A Contemplative Guide, Gouverneur Mosher, Charles E. Tuttle, 1964. Idiosyncratic guide to a personal selection of Kyoto's best sites.

Japanese Religion: A Survey by the Agency for Cultural Affairs, Kodansha International, 1972. As dry as it sounds, but reliable and comprehensive on Buddhism, Shinto, new religions and much else.

Index

Akihito, Emperor 24
Ame-no-koyane-no-mikoto 54
Ameterasu-Omikami 24, 120
Amida *see* Buddha
Amida-do, Higashi-Honganji 96
Angkor Wat monument, Cambodia 16
animistic cults 9, 22
Ashikaga family 65, 101, 102
Ashikaga Yoshimasa 102
Ashikaga Yoshimitsu 101
Asuka period art 40

Basho 115
Beijing 56, 74
Bishamon 71
Bishamonten 43
Biwa, Lake 73
Boat Docking Room, Hiunkaku 96
Bodhisattvas 40, 43, 71
Borabudur monument, Java 16
Buddha 36, 40, 43,54, 56-7, 59, 70, 71, 83, 112
    Amida (Lord of the Western Paradise) 74, 77, 79, 86, 94, 96
    of the Diamond World 71
    Dainichi 71
    of the Future 43
    Kongo-kai 71
    of Medicine 40
    Shakyamuni 35, 40, 43, 79, 88, 94, 109
Buddha Hall 83, 90
    Daitokuji 88, 90
    Horyuji 36, 40
    Kamakura 112
    Nanzenji 83
    Todaiji 44, 47, 56, 57, 59, 112, 120
    Toji 73
    Toshodaiji 50
    Yakushiji 46, 49
Buddhism
    architecture 9, 12, 30, 33, 35-6, 66, 67, 86, 96, 115, 118, 120
    history of 9, 12, 16, 19, 22, 35, 49, 54, 61-81
    pilgrimages 52, 54
    schools of 12, 71, 74, 78, 79, 94
Butsuden (Buddha Hall), Nanzenji 83
Byodo-in (Temple of Equality), Uji 14, 65, 72-7, 101

Cambodia 16
China
    architecture 15, 21, 30, 36, 81, 83, 90, 101
    cultural influence 12, 19, 24, 33, 35-6, 49, 50, 70, 74, 81

Chion-in temple, Kyoto 94
Chogen 57, 59
Chokushi-mon 88
Chugi-ji 43
cormorant fishing 77
creation myths 22

Daibutsu (Great Buddha), Kamakura 10, 112
Daibutsuden (Buddha Hall), Todaiji 56
Daigoku-den (Hall of State), Kyoto 66
Daisen-in sub-temple, Daitokuji 92
Daito Kokushi 88
Daitokuji temple, Kyoto 15, 33, 65-6, 88-92, 109
Dannoura, battle of 79
double roof technique 46

earthquakes 19, 109
Edo period 9, 30, 83, 120
Eiga Monogatari 74
Eiheiji 115
Eikan-do temple, Nanzenji 86, 102
Enchin 67, 69
Engakuji (Enkakuji) temple, Kamkura 109
Enryaku-ji temples, Kyoto 71, 90

Five Wrathful Gods 71
Fujiwara family 50, 52, 54, 65, 73-4, 77
Fujiwara Michinaga 73-4
Fujiwara Yorimichi 74
Futsunishi-no-mikoto 54

Ganjin (Chien-chên) 49, 50
gardens 21, 86, 92, 102, 112
    'dry' style 92
    rock 92, 94, 102
Gate of Sunlight, Nikko 120
Ginkakuji (Temple of the Silver Pavilion), Kyoto 15, 33, 61, 65, 83, 100-2
Go-Daigo, Emperor 88
Gojo Bridge, Kyoto 92
Golden Hall
    Horyuji 35, 40
    Kofukuji 52
Goshirakawa, Emperor 78
Great Kanto Earthquake (1923) 19, 109
Group of Guardians (Hachibu-shu) statues 52
Guardian Kings of the Four Quarters 43

Hachiman (God of War) 105
Hachiman-gu shrine, Kamakura 105-8, 118
Hall of State, Kyoto 66, 77
Hall of Worship, Toshogu 118
Hasedera temple, Kamakura 112
Hatto (Dharma Hall), Nanzenji 83
Hatto (Lecture Hall), Daitokuji 88, 90
Heian Jingu shrine, Kyoto 66
Heian-kyo *see* Kyoto
Heijo-kyo *see* Kofukuji
Heike clan *see* Taira clan
Hideyoshi 73, 88, 96
Hiei, Mount 65, 67, 71, 73, 90
Higashi-Honganji temple, Kyoto 33, 66, 96
Higurashi-mon (End-of-day Gate), Nishi-Honganji 96, 118
Hill of Cranes, Kamakura 105, 106
Hime-gami 54
Hitokoto (Single-utterance) Kannon 52, 54
Hiunkaku (Floating Cloud Pavilion), Nishi-Honganji 96
Hojo (Abbot's Quarters), Daitokuji 88, 90, 92
Hojo family 12, 109
Hojoji temple 74
Holy of Holies, Nikko 120
Hon-do, Kiyomizudera 67, 69
Honen 94
Honganji temple, Yamashina 94
Horyuji temple, Nara 4, 9, 32-43, 46, 50, 69, 120
Hosso sect 69
house, styles of 19, 21-2

Iemitsu 118
Ieyasu 83, 118, 120
    mausoleum 9, 11, 12, 118
Ikaruga 33
Ikkyu 92
India
    architecture 57, 86
    and Buddhism 9
Inner Gate, Horyuji 35, 36
Inner Shrine, Ise 24, 29
Ise shrines 18-22, 24, 27, 29-30, 106, 120
Izumo Taisha shrine, Shimane 24, 30, 54

Japan
    and foreign culture 35
    modern 15-16, 50, 61
Japan Alps 73
Java 16
Jimmu, Emperor 22

Jizo 48, 91, 112
Jocho 77
Jodo Shin sect 65, 66, 86, 94, 112
Jodu Shin-shu (True Pure Land) sect 94
Jodo Shu (Pure Land) sect 94
Jomon period 21
Joshu's Dog 81
Juko-in, Daitokuji 92

Kamakura 12, 56, 79, 81, 83, 94, 105-12
Kameyama, Emperor 83, 86
kami 22
Kammu, Emperor 59, 61, 63, 65, 66, 70
Kamo River 63
Kannon (Goddess of Mercy) 40, 50, 67, 78, 79, 112
Kano Tanyu 90
karayo 81
karesansui 92
Kasuga Taisha shrine, Kofukuji 53-56, 58
Kasuga-zukuri building style 54
Katsura Rikkyu imperial villa 16
Kenchoji temple, Kamakura 104, 107, 109
Kimon (Devil's Gate), Kyoto 71
Kinkakuji 101
Kinkakuji (Temple of the Golden Pavilion), Kyoto 15, 33, 60, 61, 65, 101-3
kitsune 106
Kiyomizu Zaka (Teapot Lane), Kyoto 69
Kiyomizudera temple, Kyoto 65, 66-9, 70
Kiyomori 78, 79
koan 81, 109
Kobo Daishi *see* Kukai
Kobori Enshu 92
Kodo (Lecture Hall), Toji 70
Kofukuji temple, Nara 17, 48, 50, 51, 52, 56, 69, 77, 86
Kogetsu-dai (Moon-viewing platform), Ginkakuji 102
Koho-an, Daitokuji 92
kojiki 22
Koken, Emperor 49
Kondo 40
Korea
    architecture 15
    cultural influence 35, 43
    religion 22
Koya, Mount 65
Koyasu (Easy Child) Kannon 69
Kudara (Korean) Kannon 43
Kukai (Kobo Daishi) 70, 71, 86
Kyogokuji *see* Toji

Kyoho-chi pond, Kinkakuji 101
Kyoto (Heian)
    as capital city 9, 12, 24, 56, 59
    city design 61, 63, 65, 71
    Prefecture 50
    temples 15, 33, 61-104

Lecture Hall
    Daitokuji 88, 90
    Horyuji 35, 36
    Shittenoji 36
    Toji 70

MacArthur, General 15
Mahayana Buddhism 71
meditation 79, 81, 94, 109
Meiji period 19, 35, 52
Minamoto clan 57, 77-9, 105, 109
Miroku 43
Mishima, Yukio 101
Momoyama period 69
Muromachi period 101
Myohonji temple, Kamakura 112

Nagaoka 59
Nandaimon 13, 36
Nanendo sub-temple, Kofukuji 51, 52, 69
Nanzen-in (Main Hall), Nanzenji 83, 86
Nanzenji temple, Kyoto 15, 33, 65, 80-88, 102, 109
Nara
    site and status 21, 56, 59, 61
    temples 9, 15, 16, 33, 43, 49, 50, 52, 59
Nara Park 50
Neo-Confucianism 12
Nichiren sect 94, 112, 115
Nihon Shoki 24, 29, 35
Nikko 9, 96, 111-15, 118, 120
Nishi-Honganji temple, Kyoto 14, 33, 66, 96-9, 118
Nishinokyo 49, 50
Nobunaga, Oda 73
Northern Octagonal Hall, Kofukuji 52

Oku-no-In (Deep Shrine) 118
Onamochi 24
Osaka 36
Outer Shrine, Ise 20, 23, 24, 26

Paekche 35
pagodas 35-6, 112

Horyuji 35-6, 40
Kofukuji 52
Nanzenji 86
Nikko 118
Shittenoji 36
Toji 70
Yakushiji 43, 46, 49, 52
'paradises' 74
Philosopher's Path 83, 102
Phoenix Hall, Byodo-in 14, 72-7, 79
Picture Hall, Yakushiji 49
pilgrimages 52, 54
pit-houses 21

Record of Ancient Things 22
Rengeji, Kyoto 89
restoration work 16, 49, 61, 74
Rikkyu 88
Rinzai school of Zen 81, 92
ritual purity 24
Ryoanji temple, Kyoto 15, 92-5, 120

Sado Island 115
Saga 70
Sai Mon (West Gate), Kyoto 69
Saicho 71
Saiji (West) temple, Kyoto 63, 70-3
Sammon (Triple Gate) 83, 88
samurai 77-8, 83
Sanjusangendo temple, Kyoto 78
Sekka-tei, Kinkakuji 102
Sembon Dori 63
Sen-no-Rikyu 88, 92
Seoul 74
Shaka-do (Buddha Hall), Toji 73
Shakyamuni *see* Buddha
shamanism 22
Shariden (Relic Hall), Engakuji 109
Shimane Prefecture 24
Shinden-zukuri style 101
Shingon sect 12, 65, 70, 79, 86
Shinju-an, Daitokuji 92
Shinran 94, 96
Shinto
    architecture 12, 118
    beliefs 24, 105
    history of 9, 12, 22, 54
    shrines 16, 22, 24, 29-30, 66, 105-6
Shitenno (Four Heavenly Kings) 71

Shittenoji temple, Osaka 36, 70, 83
shoguns 69
Shoko-do (Refectory), Toji 71
Shoma, Emperor 49
Shosoin storehouse, Todaiji 50
Shotoku, Prince 9, 12, 35, 40, 43
Shunjo-do, Todaiji 57
Soka Gakkai 112
Soper, Alexander 115
Soshi 112
Soto Zen temple, Eiheiji 115
South Great Gate
    Kofukuji 52
    Shittenoji 36
    Todaiji 56, 57
    Toji 70
    Toshodaiji 49-50
Southern Octagonal Hall, Kofukuji 52
Suiko, Empress 35
Suinin, Emperor 29
Sujun, Emperor 29
sukiya 96
Sun Goddess 22, 24, 29, 120
Sung period 57
Suzaku Oji, Kyoto 63

tahoto 86
T'ai-ho-tien palace, Beijing 56
Taian-ji (Gentle Delivery) temple, Kiyomizu 69
Taira (Heike) clan 57, 77-9, 105
Taishi-do (Founders Hall)
    Higashi-Honganji 96
    Toji 71
    Zuisenji 112
Takemikazuchi-no-mikoto 54
Tamamushi Zushi (Beetle-wing Shrine) 40
Tamura-do, Kiyomizudera 67
Tamuramaro, Saka-no-ue ('Top-of-the-hill') 67, 69
T'ang dynasty 15, 33, 52, 63, 77
Tankei 78
Tanzan Shrine, Nara 41
Tao-Lung (Daigaku-zenji) 109
tea ceremony and rooms 15, 88, 92, 96, 102
temple bracketing 46, 48, 50, 57, 59, 90, 120
Tempyo era 49
Tendai sect 12, 65, 67, 71, 79, 86, 90
Tenjikuyo 57
Teshigahara, Hiroshi 88
Thirty-three Temple pilgrimage route 52, 69

Tibetan Buddhism 65
Todaiji (Great Eastern) temple 9, 13, 43, 44, 49, 50, 56-9, 120
Todogawa River 67
Toji (East) temple, Kyoto 63, 65, 70-3
Tokugawa shoguns 59
Tokyo 19, 105, 118
Tori 40
Tosho Daigongen (Buddha Incarnate, Sun God of the East) 118, 120
Toshodaiji temple, Nara 43, 49-50, 57, 90
Toshogu shrine, Nikko 8, 110, 113, 114, 115, 118-120
Toyouke-Omikami 24
Tsurugaoka Hachiman-gu shrine see Hachiman-gu shrine, Kamakura

Uji 74, 77

Wakamiya shrine, Kamakura 106
Wakamiya-oji, Kamakura 105
warriors see samurai
Western culture, influence of 35
World War II 15, 61

Yakushi 40
Yakushiji temple, Nara 16, 42-9, 50, 69
Yamashina 94
Yamato 21, 33, 35
Yamato-no-okunidama-no-kami 29
Yayoi period 21-2, 29
Yomei-mon, Nikko 120
Yoritomo 79, 105, 106
Yoshitomo 78
Yumedono Hall, Horyuji 40
Yuryaku, Emperor 29

Zen (Cha'n) sect 12, 15, 65, 77-81, 83, 88, 90, 92, 94, 109
    architecture 81-94, 101, 109
Zuisenji temple, Kamkura 112
Zuishin-in temple, 64